A MAN ON PURPOSE

"Every man longs for a father who can teach him what it means to be a man, a true man who lives with purpose and freedom. In *A Man on Purpose*, Pete Burak shares powerful lessons not only from his own father but, more importantly, from God the Father. This book is a profound guide for men to discover or rediscover their true identity and calling as God's beloved sons. From the introduction to the conclusion, Pete's words lead me further into the heart of God, connecting with my deepest desire to know my heavenly Father and my mission in life."

Paul George
Author of *Holy Grit: A Saintly Guide to Becoming a Man of Virtue*

"I'm grateful for this wisdom-filled book from Pete Burak. Navigating the modern world is no easy task, and *A Man on Purpose* provides a field guide of stories and practical tips for anyone looking for solid ground to build a life on. With insights that reflect the heart of God the Father, Pete is leading an expedition to holiness—and I am happily following him."

Liv Harrison
Catholic speaker and evangelist

"There is a crisis of manhood and fatherhood today. As men struggle with important questions—from who they are to what they are made for—Burak's book provides answers and offers hope. *A Man on Purpose* is an engaging and enriching read. I recommend it to this generation of young men and fathers alike!"

Curtis Martin
Founder and CEO of FOCUS

"This book comes from the heart of a man who lives what he teaches. Pete is a gifted teacher, author, and leader; he is also, in my personal experience, a heroic husband and father. Within these pages, you'll not only find inspiration for becoming a saintly man, father, or grandfather—you'll discover practical, hard-won wisdom for becoming the man you were created to be and guiding the young men in your life to do the same. I give this book my highest recommendation."

John Bishop
Founder and executive director of FORGE

A MAN ON PURPOSE

10 Rules of Life from a Faithful Father

PETE BURAK

Ave Maria Press Notre Dame, Indiana

Founded in 1865, Ave Maria Press is a ministry of the United States Province of Holy Cross.

www.avemariapress.com

Paperback: ISBN-13 978-1-64680-441-2

E-book: ISBN-13 978-1-64680-442-9

Cover and text design by Christopher D. Tobin.

Printed and bound in the United States of America.

Library of Congress Cataloging-in-Publication Data is available.

In memory of the man who taught me
what it means to be a man of God.
Thanks, Dad. I love you.

And behold, a voice from heaven,
saying, "This is my beloved Son, with
whom I am well pleased."
—Matthew 3:17

CONTENTS

FOREWORD

by Jake Khym

I'll never forget the day my son Judah wanted to exercise with me. My plan was simple but intense: repeated sprints up a long, steep hill outside our house. I had already run it a time or two and was gasping for breath when Judah, just eight years old, asked to join me.

Part of me hesitated—he looked a little overwhelmed but also eager to face a challenge. I gave him a little pep talk before the run and encouraged him to push through the pain and fight past the urge to quit. About halfway up, I slowed, suddenly unsure if this was too much for him. But Judah kept going. My heart swelled with pride at his grit, even as I saw how hard he was struggling. He gutted it out, made it to the top, and then, with labored breaths, said, "Dad, I don't feel good." A few steps later, he threw up all over the driveway. He was scared and overwhelmed by the rush of dizziness and nausea. He wanted to go inside.

In that moment, I felt crushed. Was this fatherhood? Had I inspired my son or scarred him? Shame, doubt, and regret hit me all at once. Did I push him too hard? Did I miss the point entirely?

And truthfully—I had. Before going outside to do the hill sprints, I had been harshly chastising my kids for being "lazy." Also, Judah battled severe asthma as a young boy, a condition that had nearly taken his life more than once. Looking back, it's clear I missed what really mattered that day.

Judah didn't just want to conquer a hill. He wanted to be with me. He wanted my approval, my blessing, my pride. He wanted to know he had what it took, and that his dad saw it. That's what every son longs for. But I was blinded by my own agenda—my plans, my outcomes—rather than attentive to my son's heart.

If you're a father, you probably know this feeling. You want to get it right. You try hard. And still, there are times when you end up overwhelming, dismissing, or even wounding your child. Despite the fronts we put up, shame creeps in. We wonder if we're doing enough, or if we're failing at the most important task we've been given. Some of us excuse it. Others beat ourselves up. Some fade into the background because there's no teleprompter for fatherhood. No script to tell us what to do. We stumble. We second-guess. Sometimes we get it right; sometimes we don't.

Fatherhood is hard. And that's exactly why this book matters.

Pete Burak has written something every father and son need—not because it offers a formula, but because it offers a path. It's filled with stories, lessons, and practices born out of the real journey of being a son and becoming a father. With honesty, humor, and humility, Pete shows us the places he's been broken, the moments he's been called higher, and the ways life formed him—through his own dad, through other men, and ultimately through God the Father.

Every man knows brokenness—sometimes at the hands of our fathers, often by our own choices, frequently through shame. What we do with that brokenness makes all the difference. Pete walks beside us like a brother, offering hard-earned wisdom, pointing us back to Jesus, the one who reveals the Father.

One of the deepest truths of this book is that fathers are called to integrate their sons—but we can only do that if we ourselves are being integrated. We cannot give what we do not have. I've known Pete for years, shared ministry with him, and watched him live what he writes. He's a man who risks, who cares, who seeks to be fathered by God. And because of that, he can now father others. This book is an extension of that—Pete stepping into the role of a father to many, offering encouragement, guidance, and truth.

As you read, you'll notice Pete doesn't just inspire; he equips. He gives practical tools, covering the spectrum of identity, vision, humility, forgiveness, passion, virtue, community, sacrifice, and even suffering. He shares frameworks like the "Team Burak" pledge, simple truths that, repeated over time, shape a family's culture and give children a place to belong, grow, and mature. And he reminds us that real fatherhood isn't about being "nice." Nice is cheap. Fathers are called to be good—and goodness often demands honesty, firmness, even risk, but always for the sake of love.

I think again of Judah, doubled over after that hill run. In my shame, I wanted to hide. But fatherhood isn't about perfection, nor is it about disqualification. It's about presence, blessing, and beginning again. God is the ultimate Father. He fathers us. And as we let him, we learn to father our sons. Show me a good father, and I'll show you a man who first knew himself as a beloved son. Pete is a good father because he knows this truth—and he doesn't keep it to himself. I'm grateful.

This book is an invitation: not to avoid mistakes but to walk with Jesus, to let him shape you, and to pass that on. Pete reminds us that men who embrace the road of fatherhood will go further, and find deeper fulfillment, than men who only look to the finish line of an empty nest. Fatherhood is about walking—with God, with our sons, with our brothers.

So to every dad, every son, every man who opens these pages: Do not be afraid. If we don't father, the world will. You can do this. Risk is essential. Real strength is possible. Stop playing small. Live higher. Remember: You are a beloved son of the Father. From that identity, you are called to bless, to guide, to give life.

Let me end with a few truths that a great father once spoke to his son—truths he also passed on to me, and that echo in the words and actions of every good father. They resound from the heart of God himself:

I believe in you.

I'm behind you.

I expect great things from you.

I'm proud of you.

I love you.

May these words, and the pages that follow, father you into deeper sonship.

PREFACE

Many times I've gone on an interior rant that sounds something like this: "I don't know what to do. I don't know what to say. I don't know who to say it to. I don't feel strong enough to say it. I'm not ready!"

Jesus's consistent response to all of those statements is a resounding, "I know! That's why I've given you my Holy Spirit."

This book is a compilation of lessons I learned from my dad about what it means to be a man. Each of these stories and principles was born from the Holy Spirit empowering him to be the husband, father, and friend God called him to be. My dad attributed everything to knowing God the Father, through the Son, in the power of the Holy Spirit. I guarantee my dad's first question regarding this book would have been, "Are you going to talk about the Holy Spirit?" He regularly invited me to allow the Spirit to be unleashed in my heart, because through our baptism, we become temples of the Holy Spirit. This is miraculous!

What would our lives look like if we lived with the constant belief that the full power and majesty of God resides within us? How would the rhythms of our days change? How would our interactions with others deepen? Wouldn't our day-to-day lives take on entirely new meaning if we actually lived as if God's power was not some far-off, nebulous thing, but constantly and immediately available to us?

As we begin this journey of discovering more deeply what it means to be a man of God, please pray with me, "Come, Holy Spirit."

Though my dad continued to teach me about my need for the Holy Spirit well into adulthood, the seeds of this lesson were planted in childhood. Even though I was raised in a home steeped in real and deep faith, if you had asked nine-year-old Pete what was most important to him, he would have quickly said, "Sports!" No matter the season, I was playing something, but my greatest love was baseball. My dad played shortstop for the University of Michigan, and I wanted to be just like him. With a strong throwing arm, I regularly played both pitcher and catcher, until a slowly developing pain in my shoulder finally stopped me in my tracks. A doctor's assessment changed the course of my life. I was diagnosed with a rare condition called epiphysitis, which is a fancy word for pain. It wouldn't go away until I matured and the growth plate in my shoulder closed. Suddenly, a bomb had gone off in my happy little world. My whole identity was rooted in the pitcher's mound, and my sense of self cratered as both the emotional and physical pain increased after the diagnosis.

After several weeks of watching my struggle, my parents sat me down for a "Come to Jesus" meeting. They could see my suffering and told me that the only way to find happiness in the midst of this pain would be to offer everything to Jesus. Without much hesitation, I believed them. Their consistent witness of faith both in word and deed had laid the foundation for me to trust their invitation to follow the Lord. That night, I went into my bedroom, knelt in the classic little-kid prayer position, and said, "Jesus, I love you. Please take this suffering. I give you my life." Suddenly the skies opened, and a dove descended . . . just kidding. Nothing tangible happened. I wasn't physically healed, but as the days and weeks went by, I noticed a new peace growing in my heart. I began to believe in the reality of a good God who loved me, and I soon began having profound experiences of Jesus after receiving Holy Communion. I would come back to the pew, begin to pray, and become overwhelmed by God's presence, power, and love for me.

During one moment in prayer, I sensed Jesus asking me a question: "Pete, will you suffer for me?" Immediately, I replied, "Yes, Lord, I will." My yes translated into a remarkable string of sports injuries that lasted all the way through college: broken thumbs, ankles, and toes; a dislocated shoulder; a broken nose; separated cartilage in my rib cage; and more. I can go from the top of my head to the tips of my toes listing strains, fractures, separations, and dislocations. Each time, I would get patched up at the emergency room, where they practically knew my name, and come home to wrestle with the emotional and physical ramifications of the latest injury. Each time, my parents would gently remind me to give the suffering to Jesus and recommit my life to him. It was only through this physical suffering that I learned to lean on God, ask him questions, and listen for his answers. In emptying my heart of my own pride, the Lord was able to create room for the Holy Spirit to dwell.

My dad showed me what it was like to cooperate fully with the Holy Spirit. Through his example, I learned about my true identity, a vision for my life, humble confidence, forgiveness, and other attributes of a man of God. My hope is that by reading this book, you and the young men in your life will do the same.

INTRODUCTION

Tonight we have gathered with a few men who are truly men. They have played a special role in your life. They are here because they want to express their support for you. They want you to know that you can call on them at any time for help or advice . . . but not money.

This dinner marks the beginning of our quest to understand what it means to be a man after God's own heart. I am really looking forward to the times we will spend together discussing this subject and trying to apply what we learn to our lives.

There can't be a father on the face of the earth who is prouder or has more love for his son than I have for you.

God bless you, Pete, on your sixteenth birthday!

This was the first letter in a small binder full of them, which I received on the day I turned sixteen. These words—and the many that accompanied them—would go on to impact the rest of my life. The day had passed like any other, and I expected the happy, but usual, family fanfare in celebration that evening: my favorite dinner

(Mom's mac and cheese), a homemade birthday cake, and a few modest gifts to commemorate another year of life. But when I arrived home from school that day, I was surprised to find my dad waiting for me with cryptic instructions. "Change your shirt," he said. "We're going on an adventure."

While I was mildly surprised by the required clothing change, there was nothing unusual about us going on an adventure. Everything was an adventure for my dad. We regularly went on quests to exotic places like Meijer's grocery store, Michigan Stadium, simple hiking trails in the Botanical Gardens, or Pizza Bob's, where they served the best milkshakes in town.

We jumped into his Ford Taurus and headed off to an unknown destination. Normally very chatty, Dad drove with unusual somberness, and I didn't ask questions. We turned into the parking lot of Paesano's, one of the best Italian restaurants in the area, but this time, my dad led me around to the side door instead of the front. As we stepped into a small banquet room, I was shocked to find six of the most important men in my life waiting for me. Stunned and slightly embarrassed, I stood in the entryway of that small room and met the penetrating gazes of my Grandpa Wally, brother Brian, Uncle Ken, and two priests.

My dad turned to me and said, "Pete, it's your sixteenth birthday, and tonight we're going to talk about something very important. So, sit there and listen carefully!" Over the next few hours and plates of delicious pasta, each gentleman read a letter he had prepared to answer the solitary question of the evening: What does it mean to be a man? As each guest offered me his letter and a hug welcoming me into this brotherhood of manhood, my head continued to spin and my heart expanded. By the end of the night, my confidence was soaring.

To wrap the evening's events, my dad presented me with the rest of the letters he had collected from other men in our community and across the country. He looked me in the eye and said, "Son, we believe in you, we're behind you, and we're expecting great things from you. I'm proud of you, and I love you."

I walked out of that room empowered, slightly terrified, and exhilarated by the challenge bestowed upon me. Through their example of fatherly guidance, those men had reached into my chest, grabbed my heart, and breathed new life into me. Though not perfect or complete, I was forever different after that evening. A threshold had been crossed; a rite of passage had been experienced.

Looking back, I realize that my upbringing was unique. The men who populate this core memory didn't just write me letters on that night. They, and several others, took on active roles in all aspects of my life. They invested in my sports and academic development, and they also cared deeply about my spiritual and emotional well-being. Unbeknownst to me, my parents had conspired with the parents of my friends to become partners in the raising of their children. Who I am today is undeniably connected to the fact that the adults in my life committed to a patient and daily process of communal discipleship. Instead of relying on the nuclear family alone, our network understood the power of an extended family, and they were willing to work and sacrifice to foster those relationships.

That's why my dad called upon several of these men to welcome his son into the tribe of manhood. Many cultures throughout history have instituted a rite-of-passage moment for their adolescent boys on the cusp of adulthood. They differ across time and landscape, but their goal is similar: to help boys become men, both in their own eyes and from the perspective of the community. That dinner was one such moment, and I'll never forget it.

I grew up in what I later discovered was an exceptional Catholic family. We went to Mass every Sunday, prayed the Rosary more often than I liked, and both my parents were intentional disciples of Jesus Christ. They had given their lives to the Lord in college and determined their future family would know, love, and serve God. Prayer was a normal part of our daily life, not just before meals and major events, but as a lived experience of walking in the Spirit. Mom and Dad loved Jesus, believed his teachings, and highly valued their Catholic faith. Our family regularly served our parish community, looked for opportunities to share the Gospel, and tried to live a virtuous, holy, and joyful life together.

As distractions have increased and family structures have broken down over time, many traditional rites of passage have fallen out of fashion, if not out of practice entirely. We assume the internal character of a boy will automatically develop as his physical body matures into adulthood. But the heart of a man must be formed. He must be taught how to step into the role that society demands he fill. Far too many boys are entering an adult world that cries out for their stewardship and service, but they have no idea how to answer the call that God has put on their lives.

Whether it's the tragedy of porn addiction, the ubiquity of endless video-game playing, the lack of consistent and stable work, or the floundering of families, copious amounts of evidence demonstrate a deep rupture in the hearts of men. A world without strong men is a world that is undeniably worse for women and children. While men and women each have essential and incredible strengths, we cannot ask one to fulfill the role that God has uniquely designed for the other. So, when men fail to meet the purpose for which their Maker created them, the whole world around them suffers.

As Catholics, we have an opportunity—and a responsibility—to boldly proclaim God's design for humanity, confront the lies of the world, and provide a vision and framework for all people to flourish.

Men need to be challenged. We grow from experiences where we are tested, found lacking or worthy, and given the opportunity to respond. We require older men, not just our biological fathers, who have walked further down the path of life to look back, show us the way, lovingly correct our immature misconceptions, and beckon us toward the next step.

Men need to be led in order to know how to lead. When that example of leadership is embodied by someone who knows, loves, and is willing to sacrifice for us, we are empowered to take on those same virtuous qualities. We want to know if we're strong, capable, and worthy; we desire the pursuit of purpose and contribution.

While the encounter and response to God's call is essential for both men and women to grow in holiness, freedom, and joy, I've become increasingly aware of a particular lack of powerful Catholic masculinity. Throughout my recent travels and speaking engagements, I've observed an interesting trend. I hope my talks have inspired spiritual insights and given encouragement to the audience, but over and over again, what people—both men and women—want to talk about afterward is my sixteenth-birthday rite-of-passage experience. Fathers lament not doing something similar for their sons, and mothers eagerly ask what else my father did so they can bring tidbits back to their own families.

One particular conversation stands out. I had just wrapped a two-day mission at a small parish in Indiana, and before I could leave the front of the church, a middle-aged woman came forward to talk. She shared the devastating news that her husband of many years had suddenly decided to leave her. Of the many painful consequences of his decision, her heart was aching for her fifteen-year-old son. She asked me, "Pete, would you write a letter to him just like your father did for you?" I politely declined because of my lack of personal relationship with him, but encouraged her to ask one of his uncles, grandfathers, teachers, or other men in his life to take on the role. She agreed, but then asked, "What about a book? Do you have something I could have him read, or that I could read to help with . . . anything?"

That night, I couldn't stop thinking about this woman and her son. This boy's father had conceded his sacred responsibility to walk alongside, to help form, and to empower his child. How many other families across the world were experiencing a similar heartbreak because of a man who failed to fulfill his purpose? While I knew I wasn't the solution to this pervasive problem, I began to experience the Holy Spirit's presence around the idea of a book of lessons learned from a good father who cooperated with the Good Father.

This book is not a "How to Raise Good Sons" manual. It's a series of real, and hopefully relatable, stories that reveal and clarify principles every man needs to learn. My great hope is that the Holy Spirit will inspire each of you to take from these lessons exactly what you need in this time of your lives.

Fathers, don't allow yourselves to be tempted by despair or shame, but instead receive the conviction of the Lord to humbly learn and, if necessary, begin again, rededicated to the Lord, to your family, and especially to your children. With great blessings come great responsibilities. This is your purpose; this is your grand adventure. You can do it.

Sons, you're on the path toward authentic, mature Catholic masculinity. Lean into this process, be ready to learn, and get ready to work. If some of this seems hard, that's a good thing! It's the challenges of life that shape us into strong men so we can make things safe for those around us. The world is crying out for your unique leadership, and you have so much to offer.

Mothers, your tender strength and nurturing care is exactly what your family needs. Your God-granted ability to give generously, love fully, and suffer well will fortify the men in your life and brighten the world with the beauty that you embody. I hope these lessons will give you a deeper insight into the hearts of men, so that they may better understand yours. My dad would not have been the man, father, and husband he was without my mom. Each of these lessons flowed from their partnership, communication, intentionality, and love. She's the hidden hero of this book; I'm guessing many of you moms understand that role.

Whenever my dad went on a business trip or simply felt inspired to encourage me, he'd write a little message on a sticky note and leave it around the house for me to find.

"Take care of your mother while I'm gone."

"Keep working on your left-hand dribbling."

"I'm proud of you."

Every note always ended the same way: "Love, Dad."

I like to imagine God speaking to me in a similar way as he provides direction, assures me of his love, and encourages me to fully live the life I've been given. Our Father in heaven deeply, magnificently, and eternally loves us, and I pray you experience his love as we explore what it means to be a man after God's own heart.

1

KNOW YOUR IDENTITY

Who are you?

I opened the heavy wooden door of our Catholic high school, entered, and began to walk down the senior hallway in search of my locker. It was my first day of freshman year, and as I wove through the intimidating (and somewhat smelly) twelfth graders, I felt like I had entered a bad teen movie. Lockers rattled as a kid was pushed up against them, and I averted my eyes from a couple more focused on each other than their academics.

My walk toward locker number 208 became a perilous journey through a treacherous land of what I perceived as pure debauchery. By the time I found my locker, I was reeling as the nervous excitement of starting something new had been replaced by abject terror. I leaned my head against the cold metal and thought, "I don't think I want these kids to know that I know

Jesus." Within about three minutes on my first day of high school, I decided that my identity needed to change.

Despite my being raised in a faith-filled home, if you asked any of my freshman classmates if they had the impression that I knew Jesus, they would probably have shrugged. Throughout my freshman year, as I learned how to navigate that daily hallway of horrors, I became known as a nice guy, a good student, and a decent athlete . . . but nothing more.

I had begun to treat my faith like an old coat. As soon as I arrived at school each morning, I took Jesus off, and then on my way home, I'd put him back on so my parents wouldn't notice anything different. I tried to live with one foot in the world and one foot in the kingdom. I tried to serve two masters: Jesus and the opinions of my classmates. I became increasingly lost, confused, and shaken as my faith faded from my core identity. Jesus had given me something special, and I had replaced that gift of faith with a mix of sin, fear, and self-determination. I carried on this way until the defining moment of my early life.

It was an ordinary Wednesday, and the entire student body had gathered for our weekly all-school Mass. As usual, I sat in a hard wooden pew with a few of my good guy friends, all of whom had been raised in a similar faith environment. Father began his homily, and as usual, I zoned out. A few minutes later, I was struck by a strange feeling, as if something important was about to happen, so I sat up straighter and tuned in to what Father was saying. Suddenly, he stopped in the middle of a sentence, paused, and said, "Okay, any of you who have ever experienced God, please stand up."

A few people around the church stood, but I remained rooted to the pew. I wanted to stand. I knew I should stand. But the weight of living two different lives, consistently denying my core identity, paralyzed me.

Father, a bit perplexed by the crowd's tepid response, made it easier on us. "Any of you who have encountered God because of the beauty of the ocean or the grandeur of a mountain . . . stand up!" Now more students got on their feet, but for the second time, I remained planted in the pew.

A war was raging between my emotions and my will, and I couldn't move. Now Father, visibly concerned by the lack of response, made it even easier on us. "If you've ever had someone smile at you, or give you a really good hug, and you attributed that love to God in *any way . . . stand up*!" Now most of the congregation rose from their pews, but for the third time, I couldn't stand up. I knew I was lying, but I was too weak, scared, and confused to get on my feet. And although I felt utterly ashamed at that moment, I looked to my left and right to find that none of my guy friends had responded to the call either. If one of us had stood, all of us would have. Instead, rather than any one of us stepping up as a leader, we had all followed one another into passivity, cowardice, and shame.

One person who stood immediately when Father asked us about experiencing God was my mom. She came to every school Mass, but on this day, she stood in the back of the church, shocked by my lack of courage. On the way home from Mass, she called my dad crying and explained what she'd witnessed. "Emily," he reassured her, "this is the best thing that could ever happen to him." Then they hatched a plan to fight for their son.

When I arrived home from school that day, I found my mom sitting in the living room, her eyes still glistening from the tears she'd shed all afternoon. She posed only a single, direct question: "Why didn't you stand up?"

Embarrassed and disappointed in myself, I could only admit the truth. When asked to testify to knowing and loving the God who gave me everything, I was silent. And I didn't know why. My dad arrived a bit later, a man on a mission. Normally very cheerful, he entered the house with fire in his eyes. In spite of the guilt and confusion swirling within me, I still ended up toe-to-toe with my father. I was morose and tepid, and my dad got in my face to reignite the fire he knew existed within me. He wanted to shake me up and tap into the warrior side of the Holy Spirit. I couldn't have articulated it at the time, but internally, I was begging him for direction.

"Who are you?" he demanded to know. "Are you the man I thought you were, or some chicken shit who won't even stand up when asked if you know Jesus?"

Still, I didn't have an answer.

"Son," he said, lowering his voice, "you need to decide today what you're going to believe. You need to decide today who and what you're going to stand for."

As I met the piercing gaze of my father—the man who had always exemplified what it looked like to be a man after God's own heart—I determined that I would always stand up for Jesus.

At some point, we all experience a crisis of identity. As we leave childhood behind and enter the great wide world, we confront the questions of who we are and who we hope to become. For some, adulthood means deciding for ourselves whether to accept the belief in God ingrained in us by our parents. For others, a childhood without any coherent belief system might spur us to seek an identity rooted in something beyond ourselves for the first time. Regardless of the circumstances, every man must decide what he believes about Jesus Christ. Only then can he determine what he believes about himself.

This decision is foundational, as all of our other beliefs are built on the bedrock of our identity. While we may encounter one particularly intense moment, like the one I shared with my father, this is never just a one-time decision. Every human life entails several "identity crisis" experiences. These might be sparked by good things, such as marriage, fatherhood, or a new job, or by challenging things, like the loss of a home or the death of a loved one.

Each time one of these pivotal events occurs, we are faced with the same question: Who am I? Am I a man who freezes in fear? Am I a man who cowers from necessary conflict? Am I a man who avoids the pain of growth in favor of comfort? Or, am I a man who models my identity after the God who gave his life for me?

Fortunately, the life of the man of God is built on rock and not on shifting sands. Whenever we try to answer this question of identity without resting in God alone, we end up grasping and straining to create a world in our own image. This inevitably leads to fear, confusion, despair, and bondage. But if we look into the eyes of Jesus, we will see ourselves as he sees us, which is the correct and clearest lens for all of life.

My dad could have built his identity on so many wonderful things. He was a college baseball player and won MVP his senior year. He was a devoted husband and father. He owned a successful small business. He could beat most people on a golf course, and he raised two sons who were successful in both athletics and academics. Yet all of those things were downstream of his personal faith, hope, and love for Jesus. He stewarded these gifts well, because they all rested on the unwavering foundation of Christ.

My dad is proof that even a good thing—home, career, or family—cannot be the ultimate thing. Over time, countless voices and experiences will help shape what we believe about ourselves and the world around us. A life lived for God demands vigilance to ensure our identity is not corrupted and sacrificed on the altar of worldly pursuits.

One of the great ironies of our modern culture is the seemingly universal agreement that we're all meant to be happy, and the only way to achieve happiness is through experiencing the freedom to be our authentic selves. Instead of looking to God and the tools that his Church has given us to find clarity of identity in a confusing world, we're told to look into our own hearts, which are fickle with emotions and desires.

Through this foolish project of "self-discovery," we're encouraged to replace eternal truths with our own capricious feelings and to present them to the world for affirmation and celebration. Not only does this pattern enslave us to the sins that arise from corrupted desires, but we're also dependent on the opinions and approval of others. As we persist in this delusive framework, our true identity becomes obscured and our ability to stand for and operate in the truth is neutralized. This was my predicament during my freshman year of high school as I tried to straddle the concerns of the world and true devotion to the Lord. One foot in and one foot out left me unable to stand.

We need a savior to bring us from darkness to light, from sons of wrath to sons of God. This is how the Church understands the human condition as revealed by God through sacred scripture. We are not the heroes of our story, because the true protagonist, Jesus Christ, redeems us from our sins, sets us free, and gives us his very life. As Romans 8:11 reminds us, "If the Spirit of him who raised Jesus from the dead dwells in you, he who raised Christ Jesus from the dead will give life to your mortal bodies also through his Spirit who dwells in you." St. Paul continues by addressing our deepest identity: "For all who are led by the Spirit of God are sons of God. For you did not receive the spirit of slavery to fall back into fear, but you have received the spirit of sonship. When we cry, 'Abba! Father!' it is the Spirit himself bearing witness with our spirit that we are children of God" (Romans 8:14–16).

Do you believe this? Have you accepted God's love into your heart, asked him to forgive your sins, and decided to live for him? Have you given your life to Jesus Christ?

The road to mature Christian manhood begins and ends with the joyful knowledge of who we are in Christ. Sometimes the Lord uses difficult moments to remind us of our true and eternal identity. Do not fear; run to your good Father—he's always ready to catch you.

On that fateful day when I was fourteen years old, my dad asked me if I was a coward or a man who would stand up for Jesus. The memory of that moment still shakes me up, because my dad meant for it to do just that. Now, you are faced with the same question. Will you embrace your identity as a beloved son of God?

2

CAST VISION

You're a bunch of losers.

Preseason conditioning had started, open-gym scrimmages were revealing the talent of our new team, and the four seniors brimmed with confidence. This was our year. Boys' basketball at Fr. Gabriel Richard High School had suffered through a decade of mediocrity, but this season would be different.

A long string of losing seasons convinced us that we were due for a league championship victory. We had talent, confidence, a new coach, a dynamic new freshman forward, and we knew it was our time to shine.

After a few weeks of listening to our bombastic prognostications and watching our practices—the intensity level of which didn't quite match up with our belief in an imminent win—my dad decided we needed a healthy dose of reality. He told me to grab the other seniors and meet him at our house after school.

Buoyed by our adolescent egos, we gathered in my family's basement lounge, ready to hear my dad echo our enthusiasm for the season ahead. Instead, he greeted us with a declaration: "Boys, you're a bunch of losers."

We were shocked. Had he not gotten the memo that fate alone owed us a win? We all slumped as he continued, gripping an official-looking manila folder in his left hand. "You guys haven't won anything yet, but you're acting like a championship is a given. You have not earned the right to think or talk that way."

Then he opened the folder and handed each of us a sheet of paper listing the data he had compiled. "Here's your recent record against every team on your schedule: Shrine: 0–18 in the last 9 years, Bishop Foley: 2–14 . . ." He went through each team, demonstrating our losing record against every single one.

He informed us that, given the stats, every team on our schedule had our game circled as a guaranteed victory . . . for them. In that moment—despite the youthful hubris that had us flying high over the last few weeks—we were, in fact, losers. But we didn't have to stay that way.

"Well?" my dad asked. "What are you going to do about it?"

Silence filled the basement as we contemplated this tough-to-swallow description of our upcoming basketball season. Our accomplishments didn't match our bravado, and our false confidence had slowly blurred our focus and softened the edge of our training. That afternoon, we were confronted with a vision of ourselves as we truly were. That humbling conversation with my dad filled us with determination, sober confidence, and a willingness to work harder than we ever had. Before, we'd simply had a lofty desire. Now, we had a goal, and we intended to take every step necessary to achieve it. We even printed warm-up shirts with "Winners or Losers?" on the back to remind us of the mountain we wanted to climb and the effort required to reach its summit.

From high school basketball teams to religious circles to the secular realm of business, the concept of "living with a vision" has come to mean many different things. While the material world encourages us to envision the future as defined by the superficial things that populate it, a God-centered worldview enables a man to discern a vision for his faith-filled family, purposeful career, and meaningful contributions to the world. Determining the vision for one's life requires responding to a seemingly simple question whose answer is all too often elusive: What is God's plan for me?

The Lord's vision for us starts with an assurance of our identity, which is always and ever rooted in Christ. When we firmly plant our feet on that foundation and work to align our free will with God's will for us, his good plans are gradually revealed. Making life's consequential decisions can feel daunting as we look toward the big vision of our future. We may begin to worry that one misstep could throw the whole plan off track, but we must be careful to remember that the path to reaching our big dreams is traveled one small step at a time. If we focus solely on the destination instead of creating a realistic map for how to get there—just as my teammates and I were thinking only of winning a championship without considering a realistic approach toward achieving victory—we'll lose sight of the day-to-day adventure the Lord invites us to enjoy. Living in harmony with our God-given identity and pursuing his plan for our lives does not guarantee that there won't be challenges or even setbacks, as failures force us to redirect or begin again. Like the victories, our daily struggles reinforce our identity, clarify our goals, and invite us to live each day with intention.

This is why the story of Gideon is one of my favorites in the Old Testament. During this time, the Israelites were being harassed and abused by a tribe called the Midianites. As they had before, the people of Israel had forgotten their identity as the Chosen People and begun to worship false idols. Removed from the Lord's blessing and protection, they succumbed to the oppressive influence of the Midianites. Instead of destroying the Israelites, who had no capacity to protect themselves, the Midianites waited for them to grow crops, then swept in and stole the results of the Israelites' hard work.

When we first encounter the Israelite Gideon, he is threshing grain in his house. Full disclosure: I have never threshed grain, but I've spoken to those who have. I'm told this is not an indoor activity, because of the chaff and dust generated by the threshing process. So why is Gideon working inside his house, rather than outdoors? Because he's scared. He knows if he threshes the grain outside, the Midianites will see him and steal the fruits of his labor. In the midst of this cowardly activity, Gideon encounters an angel of the Lord. Rather than admonish him for his fearfulness, though, God's messenger greets Gideon with the words "you mighty man of valor" (Judges 6:12). But wait a minute. No, he's not! He's a little scaredy-cat. The angel is reminding him who he truly is: a son of Israel, one of God's Chosen People, and therefore called to be rooted in courage, rather than fear.

The angel then gives Gideon an incredible mission: to free the people of Israel from the oppression of the Midianites. Strengthened by the reminder of his true identity in the Lord, Gideon embarks on the journey of freeing his people, beginning with repenting by tearing down the idols of the false gods the Israelites were worshipping. But, still afraid, he does this under the cover of night. Isn't that encouraging to us today? Even as he begins to walk in his true identity, Gideon still deals with fear and doubt.

After the destruction of their false idols, the men of Israel rally by the thousands to join Gideon in battle against their oppressors. Suddenly he has an army, but the Lord then instructs Gideon to send away roughly 95 percent of them. Remarkably, he trusts enough to obey and moves forward with great courage. He's no longer afraid. He knows who he is and what to do—whatever God says—even if it means cutting his army by the thousands. Through this process of believing in his true identity, repenting, and walking in faith, Gideon eventually leads only three hundred Israelites to victory over the entire Midianite tribe.

Men don't want to live in fear, merely surviving each day. We don't want to be simply managed or corralled. We yearn for a compelling vision, to be stretched beyond our natural inclinations and assured that we are capable, strong, and worthy. We love an inspiring rallying cry, words used to name that innate need for identity and purpose that is written on our hearts.

Somewhere along the way, my parents started calling our little family Team Burak. Team Burak was always present, cheering from the bleachers at one another's games. Or, in my case, as the batboy for my older brother Brian's varsity baseball team. The members of Team Burak loved and respected each other, so even though Brian could have teased me and beat me up at any point, he didn't . . . usually. Team Burak loved the Lord and his people, so we never missed Mass and looked for ways to serve the community. Team Burak forgave quickly, embraced adventure, and stuck together, in times of both struggle and triumph. My parents intentionally fostered a clear and consistent vision for our family; its strength held us steady through each day and gave us a home base to find again if we lost our way. It was a "sticky" vision, easy to remember, and fun to say. We're Team Burak, and if you ever find yourself at my mom's table for a family dinner, you'll feel the bright warmth of that identity that's carried our family through generations.

The names we call ourselves matter. They are indicators of what we believe and value. Without God's vision, we are destined to move through this life like a blind man stumbling through dark woods in search of his identity—wayward, alone, and struggling to find our way. There will be times when God's light surprises us, revealing how lost in the darkness we've become. It may sting when the light hits our eyes, but opening them to the Lord's vision is always better than remaining hidden in the shadows.

It didn't feel great when my dad told my senior basketball buddies and me that we were a bunch of losers, but it was a truth that we needed to hear. After dusting off our bruised egos, we acknowledged reality and created a new vision for ourselves. With our goal in mind and a newly humble approach to how to achieve it, we started the regular season slowly with some minor wins and some very bad losses. We didn't quit or give in to despair. We just kept casting the vision, and eventually things began to click. We barreled into the Catholic league playoffs on a winning streak until the semifinals against Bishop Foley, the third-ranked team in the state.

After an intense overtime victory (*Holy moly, we beat Foley!*), we won the league championship, finishing the season with our heads held high because we earned the right to see ourselves as winners. A new vision was established for future teams, and it all started because my dad had the courage to call our inflated egos into question and make us confront who we really were.

To this day, I often turn to the Lord in prayer and say, "Jesus, let the real me encounter the real you." If we ask in the right posture, God gives us the eyes to see things as he sees them. Only in that vision can we live the fullness of what he has planned for us.

3

HUMBLE CONFIDENCE WINS

If you lead, they will follow.

Mr. Stout's gravelly, gruff voice morphed into an impressive bellow. "Let's go, ninth graders!" Forty-five boys surged forward as the camp activities director began running down the path.

"Two lines, I need two lines," he instructed, as we struggled to keep up with his pace. Pine Hills Boys' Camp had begun, and these kids were about to get their first taste of the misleadingly named "Milk and Cookies."

Each summer, seventh-, eighth-, and ninth-grade boys register to experience the three goals of Pine Hills Boys' Camp:

1. Encounter the personal love of Jesus in the power of the Holy Spirit.

2. Experience and learn Christian masculine leadership.

3. Have a ton of fun.

Organized into small groups called squads and led by adult counselors, each grade level contributes differently to make camp great. The ninth graders face the most difficult challenge of being forged into a group capable of leading their younger fellow campers. The instructional method of this formation includes some teaching, lots of apprenticeship from the counselors, and times of immersion where the ninth graders metaphorically have to either sink or swim. Every element is intentional, and every facet is designed to help young men experience, learn, and experiment with what it means to be a Christlike leader. Milk and Cookies, a name designed to disguise the actual activities endured, is a daily morning workout where the ninth graders are pushed physically and trained as leaders.

As a kid, I watched my brother Brian attend camp for years, and I couldn't wait to embark upon the adventure myself. Brian won the prestigious Leadership Award his ninth-grade year, and seeing my dad burst with pride at his son's recognition confirmed that I would shoot for the same honor when my turn came. Dad made it clear that leadership was part of what it meant to be a Burak man; I was no exception.

As a ninth grader in 2002, I knew camp would be more difficult than my seventh- and eighth-grade years, but I didn't anticipate just how hard it would be. A few days into the week, I was struggling with both the physical and mental challenges of being at the top of the camp food chain. Whether it reflected reality or not, I perceived the weight of everyone's expectations of who and how I should be as a leader, and the burden felt too heavy to carry.

The camp director, Mr. Newville, wisely assessed my angst and took me for a little walk-and-talk. He started with kind and specific affirmations of me as a young man, disciple of Jesus, and friend. After building up my confidence, Mr. Newville suddenly stopped walking. He turned, looked at me directly, and sternly—but gently—challenged me to step into my new role as a leader. He explained that leadership seemed hard because it *was* hard, and that the burden I felt was completely natural. It was a good thing that I carried the weight of expectations; it meant that I was taking the responsibility seriously. Now, I was presented with a choice. I could either rise to the occasion and accept the growth challenges of leadership, or I could shrink back, be comfortable, and ride out the remainder of the week just like I had every other summer. He challenged me to ask Jesus for the power and grace to accept this opportunity, and I decided to go for it.

One of the adages my parents drilled into me for as long as I can remember is "If you lead, they will follow." Early on, I wasn't sure what it meant to lead, and I didn't know who these elusive followers were, but it was such a consistent mantra that I found myself believing it. Around third grade, I began to notice that other people tended to listen to my perspective and were sometimes even influenced by my behavior. I started to become more aware of how the words I spoke and the decisions I made could impact others, for better or worse. I began to contemplate what being a good leader actually entailed.

Leadership is sometimes misunderstood as simply the willingness to act first, or the inclination to shout in order to be the loudest voice in the room. Magnanimous influence, innovative ideas, and judicious vocal authority are certainly aspects of leadership, but one of the most important traits that boys need to develop as they mature into manhood is humble confidence.

Think of some examples of strong leadership you've observed in our society. In sports or business, the military or politics, you're sure to find that this particular combination of humility and confidence sets the exceptional leaders apart from the adequate ones. A star quarterback cannot make it to the Super Bowl without relying on the athletic strength of his teammates; a lawmaker cannot pursue what's best for his constituency while neglecting collaboration with his colleagues. Across industries, great leaders are confident in their skills and abilities but humble enough to learn from and cooperate with others.

We may not all end up with our names in the Hall of Fame or the halls of Congress, but all men are called to lead in some way. Inspired by examples of great leadership, whether on the global stage or in our own communities, we can begin to examine our lives and question how we can step into leadership roles to positively impact those around us. Can we take on additional responsibilities at work in order to make systems run more smoothly? Or perhaps we might finally address those pesky home repairs that have been lingering for far too long. Taking initiative even in small ways will help fortify our strength of character for the ultimate and universal responsibility to which all baptized disciples are called: leading ourselves and others to Christ.

We're all invited to utilize our gifts, not just for our own self-improvement, but for the betterment of others. This is more than a mere attitude; it is a developed skill and mindset that will shift our entire worldview. When we begin with the foundation of securing our identities in Christ alone and establishing a vision for our lives, then we can identify the innate gifts that have been handed to us from the Lord. In gratitude for his offering of these talents and skills, we can work to develop them, refining our passions into areas of expertise. Sure, it feels good to become excellent at something, but our remembrance of Christ's sacrifice on the Cross invites us to follow his example of humility. In doing so, we pursue excellence only so that we may better serve others and thereby worship God.

This mindset is radically opposed to how the world tells us to regard ourselves and our purpose. As a result, maintaining humble confidence can feel like a constant tug-of-war between our own selfish desires and delusions of grandeur—which the world encourages—and the life that God calls us to live. As important as it is to resist the sin of pride, we must also be careful to discern the difference between being humble and belittling ourselves. The great Christian writer and scholar C. S. Lewis said that "humility is not thinking less of yourself, it is thinking of yourself less." Humility isn't acting as though you're no good, weak, or lacking talents. Rather, a humble man recognizes his gifts and strengths, honestly acknowledges God as their origin, and then looks to maximize them, not for his own glory, but to bless those around him. A humble man of God understands his weaknesses but isn't deterred by them, for he knows God has equipped him for an eternal mission.

In 2 Corinthians, St. Paul implores the Lord to take away the thorn in his side but learns that God has another plan: "But he said to me, 'My grace is sufficient for you, for my power is made perfect in weakness.'" Paul then confidently declares, "I will all the more gladly boast of my weaknesses, that the power of Christ may rest upon me. For the sake of Christ, then, I am content with weaknesses, insults, hardships, persecutions, and calamities; for when I am weak, then I am strong" (2 Corinthians 12:9–10).

This is one of the great dichotomies of living as a man of God. We embrace the tension between acknowledging our weakness and trusting that God's grace will fortify us to do what we cannot do alone. We believe, "I can do all things in him who strengthens me" (Philippians 4:13), because "apart from [Christ], [we] can do nothing" (John 15:5).

We're called to acknowledge our shortcomings and ask Christ to strengthen us enough to act. It's not humble to play it safe, pretend we aren't capable, or put up a front of false humility to deflect attention or responsibility. It may appear like humility to a superficial observer, but an honest self-examination will likely reveal that we're pridefully determining how and when we want to contribute, regardless of the unmet need the Lord has placed in front of us.

This was my approach at the beginning of my ninth-grade year at camp. I was playing it safe because I was afraid of being accused of trying too hard, or not trying hard enough. I was terrified of looking like I was attempting to hog the spotlight and not measuring up once the observant eyes of the other campers were turned on me. I was consumed by a worldly point of view that had everything to do with the opinions of others and very little to do with the will of God or the talents he had given me.

I knew I had gifts that would serve this new leadership role well, but I wanted control over how and when I used them. Mr. Newville helped me to see that the humble man of God gratefully accepts the Lord's gifts and lets the Holy Spirit guide him to their best use. The world doesn't need men who bashfully deflect affirmations and say, "Ah shucks, someone else should really do it," when asked to lead. Our families, communities, and churches desperately need truly humble men who know their best comes from surrendering to God's power and grace.

With my parents' consistent refrain "If you lead, they will follow," ringing in my head, and Mr. Newville's challenge burning in my heart, I began to lead that week at camp. I became more vocal at the Milk and Cookies workouts. I looked for ways to serve my squad and clarify our goals. I stood in front of the entire camp and exhorted everyone to follow Jesus. I embraced the beautiful burden of leadership and ended up receiving the Leadership Award at the end of the week, just as my older brother had. Today I'm one of the camp directors, and every summer, I keep an eye out for that one young man who isn't quite ready to embrace the leadership to which the Lord is inviting him. If not for Mr. Newville's guidance on the path of humble confidence, I don't know if I would have found the courage to step up that summer. I only hope that in attempting to use the gifts God has given me as a means of serving others and honoring him, I can encourage other young men to do the same.

4

FORGIVE QUICKLY

Will you forgive me?

Dial-up internet had arrived in the Burak house, and with it a world of possibilities, distractions, and temptations. Mom, Brian, and I gathered around the new family computer, which sat on a desk underneath the basement stairs, as Dad enthusiastically explained the capabilities of this enormous (this *was* still the early 2000s) and slightly intimidating device. Despite all the bells and whistles, my dad informed us that the primary purpose of this exciting new machine was for educational and school activities. *Age of Empires* and *Prince of Persia* would not be enjoyed without getting permission first. Brian and I readily agreed and, despite the mountain of homework we'd each brought home from school that day, proceeded to beg with great enthusiasm to play just one round of each game.

A few weeks later, I went downstairs to work on a seventh-grade novel outline. The basement's silence was punctured by the slow clack of the keys as I agonizingly spelled out every word. After several minutes, my prepubescent attention span had run out, and the ever-present allure of computer games flooded my brain. However, the temptation to open up *Minesweeper* was abruptly replaced by a totally different thought—whether the internet would have pictures of a popular female music star. Without much hesitation, I glanced around the empty basement and quickly typed her name into the search bar. You can probably guess what transpired. I knew it was wrong, but the combination of novelty, hormones, and lustful concupiscence proved too powerful, and I soon found myself trapped in a developing negative habit.

Eventually, my parents began to question my daily insistence on doing schoolwork on the computer, and before long my dad called me to the basement to talk. I hadn't known about search and website history until he gently confronted me with the evidence of my sinful behavior. I'll never forget how the rush of panicked adrenaline and the shame of being caught burned my cheeks and knotted my stomach. My dad calmly waited for me to admit to my mistakes and utter the sentences I had been taught from an early age: "I'm very sorry for doing this, and I want to do better. Will you forgive me?"

It was that last part—*Will you forgive me?*—that always threatened to stick in my throat, because it required such humility and vulnerability. "Yes, son, I forgive you, and . . ." Dad proceeded to lovingly, firmly, and clearly explain to me why these sins, while common temptations for most men, were not acceptable and needed to be battled with the grace of God. He never shamed me, nor did he act scandalized or disappointed. However, he also refused to water down the seriousness of my sin. His love, compassion, and firm adherence to the truth challenged me to grow, free to move forward with confidence and assurance that I was not defined by my sins and that my past did not dictate my future.

From the beginning, my parents instilled a process of constant forgiveness in our family. When we messed up, hurt each other, disobeyed, or experienced any other type of relational conflict, we were required to start a conversation that went something like this: "Brian, I'm very sorry for hitting you, and I don't want to do it again. Will you forgive me?" It was not enough to simply say "sorry" or promise changes. We had to actually offer those humbling and sometimes painful words—*Will you forgive me?*—and then patiently wait for a response. I can't recall a single time when this petition for forgiveness was met with a rejection, but that shouldn't come as a surprise. When we allow ourselves to see and be seen by one another in our full human vulnerability, we can't help but receive and extend compassion. One person's ask for forgiveness was always met by the other person extending it, and as was procedure in the Burak house, a hug would always follow. (I must admit, though, when it came to my brother and me, the hug was often offered begrudgingly!)

The power of this process wasn't just in the words that were spoken, but in how it was modeled by my parents, both to each other and to us. Although my mom and dad agreed on the big stuff, they often bickered about little things, such as the best route to take to an evening event or whether my dad needed to be reminded again to replace the furnace filter. (Dad always needed another reminder.) Sometimes these squabbles could get pretty heated and loud. They weren't subtle, private disagreements behind closed doors; they were held in the middle of the kitchen while I was doing homework at the counter like a silent observer. My parents weren't proud of these arguments, and they always reconciled as quickly as possible. Generally, if the tussle happened within the view and earshot of Brian and me, the process of forgiveness would be open as well. Their hug at the end always made me squirm like any self-respecting young boy would do when confronted with his parents' public displays of affection, but it impressed upon me that the need to admit wrongdoing and ask for forgiveness wasn't just something for kids, but something men and women must do their entire lives.

Extending and receiving forgiveness is essential to Christian maturity for three big reasons. First, Jesus commands us to forgive. The Our Father ties our reconciliation with God to our willingness to forgive others: "And forgive us our trespasses, as we forgive those who trespass against us." In his awesome love for us, God receives our contrition, washes us clean, and gives us the grace to begin again. The intimacy of our relationship with God means we do not need to clean ourselves up in order to come to him. Just as a child who falls off his bike does not wipe his bloodied knee before hobbling into the comforting arms of his parents, we go running to our Father's arms just as we are. Broken. Wounded. Sinful. He gathers us to himself and forgives, heals, strengthens, and restores us. Thus, we cannot put conditions on the forgiveness we offer to others. As the Father receives us with open arms, we must hold this same posture for his sons and daughters.

Some fathers have not modeled God's patience and compassionate forgiveness. Your dad may have been consistently short-tempered and frustrated with your weakness. Maybe he used shame and fear to motivate you to do the right things. Whatever your experience with your earthly father, we need to ask the Lord for grace to believe the truth about who God the Father really is and how he reacts to our weakness. God is not scandalized by our sin or impatient with our lack of progress. He never shames us. He never ignores us. When we so much as glance in his direction, he responds, no matter how many times we've sinned the exact same way before.

The second reason that forgiveness is essential to maturity is that it diminishes our temptation to create and hold a grudge. Words and behaviors from others can certainly hurt us, but when we allow resentment to set in, the wound festers and grows more painful over time. Resentment infects a wound; forgiveness is a healing balm.

Whether the person who hurt us asks for forgiveness doesn't actually matter as far as our responsibility to forgive is concerned. The act of forgiving frees us from an ongoing unhealthy connection to a negative experience or to a person who brings a negative influence to our lives. Through forgiveness, we remove whatever power they may have had over us and hand it back to the Lord. Although forgiveness often involves reconciliation with the offending party, it doesn't have to. In cases where an ongoing relationship with the person who hurt us is impossible or imprudent—such as an abuse victim choosing to forgive the abuser—we can still forgive and move forward in freedom.

Jesus modeled this for us on the Cross when he implored the Father to forgive his executioners even as they tortured and mocked him. In imitation of Christ, we need not hide from our pain or withhold our compassion from those who don't seem to understand how they've hurt us. Instead, we are called to offer our wounds and our forgiveness of those who inflicted them to be blessed by God's healing love.

Finally, when we harm other people and don't ask for their forgiveness, we erode trust and limit our ability to maintain healthy relationships. Brushing things under the rug or pretending like nothing happened feels safe in the moment but has potentially devastating costs down the road. It's difficult to admit that we've been hurt by someone, but admitting that we've hurt someone else often requires even more humility. Minimizing our wrongdoing with flippant or callous acknowledgment isn't mature or brave. It takes internal strength to admit when we've acted or spoken poorly, yet in those moments of weakness, we have the opportunity to build trust by being accountable for our actions and doing our part to make things right.

Time and time again, my father modeled this humility in asking for forgiveness. He was an amazing dad but he was also human, and his willingness to acknowledge his imperfections was one of the greatest examples of strength he showed me. I remember one particular basketball workout session with my dad that really tested his usually heroic patience. That day, we both arrived at the court in a foul mood. I missed a shot, and he sarcastically commented about my form. I muttered a snide comeback under my breath, and he snapped a pass at me harder than necessary. As the drills progressed, so did our lack of kindness toward each other until finally he snapped. My laziness, impertinence, and disrespect proved too much, and although he was totally justified in his frustration, his response was volcanic. He kicked the ball to the other side of the court, took two steps toward me, and with fury in his eyes shouted, "You're spoiled, arrogant, and I'm done coaching you today! Go pick up your ball and meet me in the car, if you're man enough and strong enough to actually go get it."

Rarely had I ever seen him so angry. I shakily went to retrieve the ball, which had rolled a considerable distance, and shuffled back to the car. Normally, our rides were lively and animated, but not today. Neither one of us had anything kind to say, so silence reigned all the way home. When we pulled into the driveway, I intended to make a quick escape to my room. Before I could, he reached over, gently gripped my arm, and said, "Pete, please look at me." I turned to him, and he had tears in his eyes. He proceeded to express how sorry he was for losing his temper, and said, "I love you—will you forgive me?" It wasn't the first time he had apologized to me and asked for forgiveness. But this time felt different. I recognized that my behavior had massively contributed to his emotional outburst. I should have been apologizing to him, but this good man took responsibility for his own actions and willingly humbled himself to begin the process of reconciliation between us. I forgave him and asked his forgiveness in return. I told him I loved him and, feeling relieved, turned to get out of the car.

He grabbed my arm again and said, "Next time we go practice, you better hustle, and don't act like an ass."

Fair enough, Dad.

Ever in pursuit of peace and justice, men of God strive to live in loving harmony with others. When discord happens and sin creeps in, men of God embrace their culpability, acknowledge where they have fallen short of holiness, and seek to restore relationships. We don't play victim, blame others, or shirk personal responsibility for our words and actions. Extending and receiving forgiveness is not optional. It is a consistent command from the Lord, and therefore it is for our good.

Ephesians 4:26 tells us to not let the sun go down on our anger. So, my friends, I implore you, don't hold grudges. Don't foster resentment. Don't pretend you haven't hurt the people in your life. Embrace the beautiful and challenging call to forgiveness. You won't regret it.

5

PURSUE PASSION

Always touch the water!

I sat in the back of my mom's purple minivan, sweaty, tired, and confused. A flimsy plastic trophy balanced on my lap; the figurine on its top was dramatically primed to kick a soccer ball. Again, I squinted at the cheap plastic plate on the bottom of the trophy: 5th Place.

The middle-school weekend tournament hadn't gone according to plan. My team lost five games and won only two, which was not normally a trophy-worthy record. I enjoyed the games and knew I had done my best, but the team clearly struggled and our place in the finishing line proved it. Yet this suspiciously light and hollow object on my lap seemed to indicate that something significant and worthy of celebration had transpired on that field.

When we arrived home, I told my dad how the team performed and showed him my new piece of hardware. Dad smiled, looked at the fifth-place designation, shook his head, and calmly deposited it in the kitchen garbage can. He then invited me into the living room for a conversation.

"Son, I've noticed you're not that good at soccer. You could be if you decided to work really hard on it. But . . . I've noticed you *are* very good at basketball. You need to work hard either way. I'll support you in whatever you decide to pursue."

That direct conversation was such a gift to me. Instead of fake celebration or empty platitudes, my dad lovingly acknowledged the positives and negatives of my athletic prowess. Most important, he gave me a choice as to how to proceed.

When you're told you're good at everything, you actually don't know what you're good at. Learning how to fail is essential to learning how to win. We want to encourage kids to get off screens and be initiators in their own lives, so handing out participation trophies or certificates isn't necessarily a bad thing if it emboldens them to take risks in new recreational activities. However, astute readers may have noticed that the trophy I received in the middle-school soccer tournament wasn't a participation trophy but a fifth-place trophy. This is an important distinction. Pseudo-validation awards and platitudes, while well intentioned, don't build confidence or inspire dedicated hard work. Failure is an essential step on the road to success, because learning from failure is vitally important in the pursuit of victory. Failure humbles us by exposing our weaknesses, but it also reveals areas of strength.

My dad didn't tell me that I wasn't good at soccer to belittle me; he did it to help me see that my real strength was on the basketball court. Youth sports, and other forms of competition like theater auditions, singing contests, or competitive debates, help prepare young people for the inevitable rises and falls of life. If boys only experience some version of victory, adulation, and affirmation, they become men who lack the experience, grit, and tools necessary to persevere when hardship sets in. It's natural for loss and disappointment to be accompanied by emotional pain, and trying to soothe the ache before it even has a chance to sting is not kindness. This only incentivizes mediocrity, neuters a boy's natural competitive instincts, and sets the wrong expectations as he enters adulthood, where the stakes involved in career, marriage, and family life are far greater than could ever be represented by the win or loss of a flimsy plastic trophy.

The big game of life isn't just about participating, because there are real consequences to the decisions we make. It might seem a stretch, but I believe there's a correlation between this "everyone is a winner" approach and the renewed cultural interest in and promotion of universalism—broadly speaking, the false belief that everyone will be saved, no matter what. This is the ultimate and eternal version of a participation trophy, and it's fundamentally not what Jesus taught or what the Catholic Church has consistently understood about salvation.

By today's standards, failure can make people feel bad, and those feelings should be minimized or avoided altogether, especially in young people. Comfort is king, no matter the consequences. This messaging contributes to a society where a bunch of guys look like men on the outside but are still little boys on the inside: lost, confused, and concerned with immediate gratification over long-term goals. They have not developed self-mastery or perseverance because they never learned how to fail, how to fight for something, or how to sacrifice for a bigger purpose.

As a father myself, I want my boys to be boys in the traditional sense. I want them to be willing to get a little dirty and scrape their knees. I want them to be so courageous and energetic that each evening's rest is a well-earned payoff for a day of adventuring in this great wide world. But, more deeply, I want them to be passionate about life. I want them to discover and zealously pursue their gifts and talents. I want them to live for something bigger than themselves. I want them to experience the delight of being on a team, where they have a role to play and aim for success as one part of a whole. I want them to understand that, while success is possible, so is failure. And that sometimes they are going to lose.

Identifying true strengths is vital. Granted, people can improve with hard work and dedication, but improvement is enhanced by supportive critique, not false flattery. Authentic confidence comes from honing in on our real God-given gifts, while a life lived in delusions of grandeur will almost assuredly lead us to assert our worth in ways that ring superficial at best and can sometimes be detrimental. I absolutely want the masculine genius to erupt in my sons, but I don't want it to get stuck in or defined by a particular cultural expression or stereotype. For instance, I don't really care how "manly" they are. It's not about whether they eventually smoke cigars, grow a beard, or work on cars. I want them to be self-sacrificial in the pursuit of noble things. I want them to live with passion, and when faced with the choice to sit on the sidelines or take the risk of getting in the arena, I want them to go for it!

My dad had an expression that I've gone on to teach my kids. It was a kind of life adage: "Always touch the water!" He believed if there was a body of water nearby, the least you could do was make the effort to go touch it. There is great truth in this simple statement. Throughout my life, I've found that if I'm willing to get out of my car to walk a trail to a river's edge, jump in an alpine lake, or jog across the sand to dip my toes in the ocean, risk, reward, and thus a great memory is always part of that experience. It was my dad's version of "seize the moment," and it has infused my life with a spirit of adventure. Now my kids know that when we're around water, I'm probably going to jump in, and I'm going to invite them to do so as well. This adage of my dad's begets a mindset that has the power to shape the course of a whole life. Whether it's an opportunity to try a new experience, start a new relationship, or take a new job, we've got to encourage our boys to dive in and enjoy the adventure that awaits them.

My dad's eagerness to participate in whatever adventure an ordinary day could hold used to perplex my brother and me. The world seemed rigid with rules designed to keep boys on their best behavior, and he was always pushing the boundary of what we thought was allowed. Dad had no qualms about taking us to Michigan Stadium to see if the gates happened to be open. Most often, they were closed, but every once in a while we would end up on the field, running routes and scoring imaginary touchdowns.

We once accompanied my dad on a work trip to North Carolina, where one of the planned corporate outings involved a long hike next to a river. Eventually, the beaten path proved too routine for our dad, and he decided to "touch the water" by climbing the massive rocks scattered haphazardly throughout the river. We followed and ended up jumping from rock to rock, working our way downstream. At one point, my foot slipped and I found myself with one leg in the river and one leg still on dry rock. Slightly uncomfortable and definitely embarrassed, I nearly started to cry until Dad smiled at me and said, "Thatta boy, now you've really touched the water!" The adventure continued for the next two hours, and our day of rock hopping embedded itself in my mind as a cherished memory.

Anything extraordinary in this life involves risk, and men thrive when we engage. Great marriage is risky. Great parenthood is risky. Great business is risky. One of my primary hopes for my sons is that they enjoy and embrace risk as a means of striving for excellence. Creating the potential of danger for its own sake is the action of an immature boy, but a man is willing to risk for a calling, a purpose, or a vision. When pursued with dignity and in honor of God, the payoff for this kind of effort is glory.

Knowing the difference between foolish and glorious risk comes down to what we discussed earlier: discerning, receiving, and embracing God's vision for your life. The ultimate version of touching the water is the pursuit of heaven. To sacrifice our time, talent, and treasure for the sake of the Gospel and intimacy with the Lord constitutes the best and most magnanimous vision of life. There is nothing more glorious than being united to God for all eternity. The innate desire in man to climb a mountain, cross an ocean, woo a beautiful woman, win the game, and conquer his fears all flow from being made in the image and likeness of God. We are designed to one day experience the fulfillment of all of our desires in him. Embracing big dreams, goals, and risks is part of what it means to be sons of God. We shouldn't suppress or ignore these desires, but instead offer them to the Lord so he can purify and clarify them.

Far too many men—even faithful ones—play the game of life at a safe half-speed, holding back ever so slightly so they can keep their options open and not risk too much. Any athlete knows that if his motivation for the game is simply not to lose, there is almost no chance of walking away with a win. When a game is played all out—no hesitation, no constraint—victory is possible. Sure, it's feasible to leave everything on the field and still lose a game, but in life, if we surrender everything we have to the Lord, we are assured of victory because it belongs to him.

Just as the Lord loves us anew each morning, seizing the day is not a one-time decision or action, but an ongoing and lifelong process. Just as everything great in life involves risk, everything worth achieving involves perseverance. The road to earthly success and eternal reward is full of twists and turns, seemingly insurmountable challenges, and dead ends. The world simultaneously celebrates the stories of those who persevere while trying to convince us we're already entitled to the destination. Resist the urge to give up, throw in the towel, or claim it's too hard. The Lord isn't calling men to be idle spectators of life, so go find some water and jump in!

6

FIND COMMUNITY

Just don't get arrested!

The closing credits rolled as my buddies and I erupted in excited analysis of the adventure we had just witnessed on the silver screen. Naturally, Zorro prevailed against his sworn enemies in spite of enormous challenges requiring cunning strategies and daring escapes. The final climactic scene was full of surprises, intense battles, and a fortuitous (if completely random) brick wall to protect our hero from the explosion meant to kill him. We could not contain our teenage enthusiasm as we raced each other through the cinema parking lot, jumped off three-foot concrete walls, and generally caused a ruckus. Our imaginations had been stimulated, the testosterone was flowing, and we needed an outlet.

We decided to swing by a classmate's house who lived nearby. As we pulled up to her house, through the big front picture window we could see the outline of her and her boyfriend watching a movie. Instantly, we hatched a plot. We raced to my house and raided my old childhood bin of dress-up clothes to look the part of daring and dangerous miscreants. As we spilled back out the front door, dressed in ill-fitting capes and masks to execute our mission, my dad yelled out, "Just don't get arrested!" My friend Mark, who was staying with us for the weekend while his parents were out of town, wasn't interested in the whole escapade, but smiled at my dad's attempt at humor. I rolled my eyes and remarked, "Pffft, what a crazy thing to say."

Our plan was simple. Half the group would creep around to the back sliding door while the other half would position themselves under the front window. At the agreed-upon moment, the backdoor crew would stand up and make noise to scare our friend and her boyfriend, then the front crew would emerge to bang on the window, thereby inducing piss-your-pants-worthy terror. It was foolproof.

We were in two cars. Our first mistake was parking very far away from the target house. It took forever to sneak through the large neighborhood, but we eventually covered the distance, and the front-window team assumed their positions. I was a member of the backdoor crew. As we began to work our way through the darkness and around the shrubbery to the appropriate spot, we were suddenly surrounded by light. We'd triggered a motion sensor! There we stood in the blinding spotlight, looking a lot less like costumed kids trying to live out their personal *Zorro* adventure and more like three large ski-masked men ready to rob the place. We froze in the driveway, but we were visible to everyone inside.

Our friend leaped to her feet and shouted, "Dad!" Panicked, we started running back to our cars, convinced the prank was unsalvageable. Blame it on the hubris of youth, but by the time we got to our parking spots (remember, very far away from the house), we had calmed down and decided we shouldn't give up so easily. Most of the guys jumped into the other car, but I told Mark to walk back and see if the coast had cleared. I planned to pull my car closer to the house so we'd have a shorter distance to cover the second time we ran for it. As I drove back toward the house, I saw our friend's dad patrolling the street with a flashlight in search of the masked men who had tripped his motion-sensor light. I whipped off my ski mask and politely waved to him as I drove by, chuckling to myself the whole time. With no sign of Mark, I assumed the other car had picked him up, but when I called the guys, they confirmed that they hadn't seen him either.

Unbeknownst to us, this neighborhood had recently been victimized by a series of home invasions, so the police were nearby. Unfortunately for Mark, he was the only one of the guys that our friend's dad didn't know. So when his flashlight beam landed on an unfamiliar dude wearing a ski mask, our friend's dad immediately pointed him out to the two police cruisers that had rushed to the scene. Mark tried to explain what had happened, but they put him in handcuffs and drove him away.

Back home, my mom's worry about our delayed return was amplified when the living room suddenly lit up with the flashing blue lights of the police cars that had pulled into our driveway. The officers came to the front door holding Mark in handcuffs and (thankfully!) released him into my mom's custody. The late-night search for our missing friend having turned out fruitless, we eventually returned home to find Mark sitting on the couch, cuff marks on his wrists, my mom looking like some combination of mostly frustrated and mildly amused, and my dad dying of laughter in the kitchen. We learned several lessons from our misadventure—including that we weren't effective pranksters—but we certainly milked our newfound notoriety as much as possible the next day at school.

Believe it or not, this ridiculous story illustrates our natural and ongoing need for community. We are not designed to move through life alone. Community is found in many forms, such as sports teams, social clubs, and workplaces—all of which have potential for amazing benefits—but a man of God needs other men who are running with him, not just in the pursuit of fun, pleasure, or common benefit, but with the highest goals of virtue and discipleship.

From leadership and a common desire for holiness to commitment and a habitual prayer practice, Christian community is steadied on multiple pillars, but one of the most vital parts of this foundation is too often lacking: a clear sense of mission. A deep, fruitful, and dynamic community cannot exist without this. As St. John Paul II writes in *Christifideles Laici*, "Communion and mission are profoundly connected with each other, they interpenetrate and mutually imply each other, to the point that *communion represents both the source and the fruit of mission: communion gives rise to mission and mission is accomplished in communion*" (32).

In a continuous loop, our communion with the Lord compels us to create communion with one another, which in turn strengthens our bond to the Lord. When we continuously pour into our relationships with God and each other, we are motivated to live missionally on this earth and bring others to Christ.

Obviously the "mission" of scaring our friend was not what John Paul II had in mind, but even this silly endeavor ultimately brought us closer together. It wasn't a particularly noble purpose, but we were focused on accomplishing something and we needed each other to do it. Men bond shoulder to shoulder better than face-to-face. If you sat most men in a circle and said, "Okay, fellas, it's time to connect with each other!" we would feel deeply uncomfortable and unwilling to engage. However, if given a task or common objective, most of us find ourselves connecting with the men around us, united in the fact that we are moving in the same direction and are all needed to accomplish a common mission.

Too many men, including Christians, feel alone right now. Their experience of church, family life, and contribution to the world has isolated them instead of drawing them into deep relationships with other believers. The game of life feels like singles tennis: *I alone have the responsibility to hit the ball over the net.* Instead, God desires that it look more like football, soccer, or hockey: everyone connected, moving, and positioning to give the entire group the chance of collective success. We talk about the Body of Christ but live like we're dismembered. And we wonder why men are lonely and unmotivated to sacrifice their time, talent, and treasure for a greater purpose!

Growing up, I knew community was vital to my parents. After all, we lived on a cul-de-sac with about fourteen other Christian families, and we attended myriad birthday parties for friends, cousins, and other relatives. However, more significantly, our parents intentionally invited other adults into their mission of raising Brian and me to know, love, and serve God. I can think of at least thirty men who cared about my spiritual life growing up, several of whom were included in that group of mentors who wrote me letters on my sixteenth birthday.

Among the many priceless gifts that my parents gave to my brother and me is the pact they made with that selected group of trusted Christian families to help raise one another's children. I could go over to family homes of the Sauters, Herbecks, Macaris, Swisses, Chockleys, Merigians, Darnells, or Rolphs and interact with men who loved Jesus, strove to follow him, and wanted me to do the same. I clearly love and admire my dad, but there were times, especially during my teen years, when I found him to be a little weird and even annoying when it came to his deeply held beliefs and moral convictions. It was incredibly powerful to see those same beliefs and morals echoed and supported by those other men, whom I also loved and admired.

When I was about thirteen years old, my dad and my friends' fathers took all of us to Northern Michigan for a retreat weekend. We stayed in one huge cabin and engaged in all the manly behavior you'd expect on a trip like that: poorly planned meals, swimming, hiking, fishing, campfires, and *super*competitive sporting activities. My friends and I were just starting to mature physically, and we felt ready to take on the old fogies with a healthy dose of competitive aggression. During one particularly intense game of flag football, I caught a beautiful touchdown pass from my friend, Jim. We celebrated, but I felt empowered to run my mouth a bit as the dads went to the other side of the field. When we got the ball back, the same thing happened, and the same mouthing off, but this time I added even more spice to it. After the game, everyone was milling about and Mr. Rolph, Jim's dad, came up to me. He looked me in the eye and said, "Pete, you're a great athlete, but you need to watch your mouth. Someday, someone is going to take exception to your taunting and you'll get what's coming to you. I'm not going to do it, but someone will." He was absolutely right, and I've never forgotten the feeling of hearing those words from him. He knew my dad would support him, and Mr. Rolph cared enough about me to deliver a hard but true lesson.

There are some things a boy won't hear from his own father but will gratefully receive from other men. When we combine our efforts and rally the gifts and insights of a community, we can speak into a young man's life from multiple angles. A communal approach to fathering young men doesn't diminish the relationship between biological fathers and sons; it strengthens it. This "tribe" approach takes on even greater significance when a young man doesn't have a biological father around, or his father is incapable of properly loving and guiding him.

Whether in my role as a mentor at Pine Hills Boys' Camp, or as an extended family member or neighbor, I consider it a tremendous privilege to be completely committed to raising my own children and also to embrace the responsibility of my role in the lives of other young people in our community. In short, we're all in this together. God calls us to support each other, encourage each other, and serve each other. Just don't get arrested.

7

LEARN TO OBEY

What's the Holy Spirit telling you?

I didn't know where to go, but I knew I had to get out of Ann Arbor. The start of my junior year at the University of Michigan was not going according to plan. The previous summer I had decided to pursue two major goals. First, building on opportunities created in the previous season, I wanted to strengthen and expand my role on the Michigan basketball team. Second, after years of discernment, I had decided to pursue the vocation of marriage.

I had offered my desire to pursue both basketball and marriage to the Lord and felt sure I was cooperating with his will. However, through a series of misunderstandings, miscommunications, and what I now see as the hand of God, my involvement with the basketball team dramatically and abruptly ended. That night, I sat alone in my apartment: hurt, confused, and angry. My dream of being a Michigan basketball player was only quasi-fulfilled, and now the path that had been so clear was shrouded in the emotional mists of rejection and loss. I admitted to God that I had agreed to suffer for him, but this wasn't anything like what I had experienced before. The deep emotional and psychological wound of this loss actually hurt like a physical injury.

Growing up, I had idolized the Michigan basketball players, and getting into that university and making the team felt like destiny. I never expected that just a few years later, I would consider transferring from U of M, but I felt it had to be done. In that pain and confusion, I turned to the Lord and asked, "Jesus, what do you want me to do?" Seemingly out of the blue, a thought popped into my head that I knew wasn't my own. The still, small voice of the Spirit replied, "Franciscan University." Huh? Isn't Franciscan in Ohio? A Wolverine couldn't possibly transfer to a school in Ohio! Do they even have a basketball team? If they do, would they even want me?

But seriously . . . Ohio?

Questions and doubts raged in opposition to where I felt the Lord was calling me, so like any distraught college student, I went home that night for my mom's homemade mac and cheese. Over the meal, I explained what I had heard in prayer and said, "But I couldn't possibly transfer at this point, right?"

"What's the Holy Spirit telling you?" my dad asked, reminding me of the prayer practice we'd instituted several years before. Whether in a season of clarity and spiritual fruitfulness, or a season of confusion and doubt—like the one I was currently muddling through—we started every morning with a simple three-word prayer: *Come, Holy Spirit.*

It was this openness modeled by my father that encouraged me to be open to God's guidance in this current moment. My dad could see the wheels turning in my head and the Holy Spirit working in my heart. "Why not email the Franciscan coach and see if the team has any room?" he asked.

Since there was no harm or commitment in making a simple inquiry, I dashed off an email to Coach Sean Donovan and assumed I might hear back in a few days. About twenty-five minutes later, he replied, saying they would be very interested in getting to know me and would welcome a chance to show me around campus. Slightly stunned, my parents and I agreed we might as well drive down to Steubenville, Ohio, and check it out.

A few days later, we parked in the flower-filled Rosary Circle at Franciscan University, where Coach Donovan greeted us. As we walked across campus, I had a startling feeling that this might actually be it. Coach brought us into Finnegan Fieldhouse to see the basketball facilities and then turned to some team pictures on the wall to point out my potential teammates. Then he showed us the women's team photo.

"Actually, two of my sisters play here," Coach said, pointing to a blonde and a brunette. Immediately, I thought, "Wow, the brunette's pretty cute." Fairly certain that a crush on his little sister wasn't going to put me in my potential new coach's good graces, I kept my thoughts to myself as the tour continued. By the end of the weekend, my parents and I felt strongly that the Lord was calling me to transfer to Franciscan. It didn't make sense academically or financially, but when it came to decision-making, my parents had taught me to lead with one basic question: What does Jesus want me to do? It sounds simple, because it is. However, answering this question honestly requires the deep faith to believe that Jesus wants to speak to us, he will speak to us, we can understand him, and we can act on what he says. After a few days of discussion, prayer, and listening to the Holy Spirit, we all decided Steubenville would be my home for the remainder of my college career.

When I arrived on campus a few months later, it was the end of Christmas break. Intimidated and nervous about this massive change, I spent the first evening reconnecting with my new coach at his campus apartment. At some point, he mentioned that one of his basketball-playing sisters had discerned a religious vocation and left the team. Immediately, I thought, "Gosh, I hope it's not the brunette!"

The next day, all the men's players were hanging out at Coach's apartment, and the topic of his sister Cait came up. (Yes, the brunette whom I had found myself thinking of, even though I'd never even met her at this point!) One of the guards, Mike, offered a warning. "She's cute, but don't bother. Coach's sister is off-limits." A few minutes later, Cait herself walked in the front door of the apartment, and—off-limits or not—I stood to introduce myself. None of the other guys even glanced up when she arrived, and she later told me that my simple gesture left quite an impression on her.

Over the next several weeks, Cait and I spent a lot of time together, and I knew I was in serious, but wonderful, trouble. We began dating, and just a few months later, Cait came to Michigan to celebrate Easter with my family. I'll never forget walking up for Holy Communion that Easter Sunday; as I approached the altar to receive Jesus, I looked around to see Cait, my parents, my pastor, and—most importantly—the massive crucifix above. I heard the Holy Spirit say, loud and clear, "She's the one." I knew it then, and I know it today. Years of marriage and five kids later, I am so thankful that I listened to God's call when he led me to Franciscan, and toward the woman who would become my wife. God knew what he was doing.

A man of God consistently asks two questions: What is God saying to me, and what am I doing about it? This attentiveness to the Lord's will is not born out of servile fear, but of the confident belief in a good Father who has a wonderful plan for our lives. Rooted in this belief, a man of God does not live for himself, but to love and serve the Lord.

Tension between rebellion and obedience is etched into the human spirit; like Adam and Eve, we must learn to choose obedience to God's will over our own rebellious nature. Despite knowing that God's plan for us is perfect, we may often find ourselves shouting toward the heavens, "Let *my* will be done!"

This is a dangerous posture for a couple of reasons. First, all sin is fundamentally a rebellion against the truth God has revealed through sacred scripture and the teaching of the Church. To disobey God places us against him, an enemy instead of his beloved son. All the baptized now belong to God's family, but through free will, we can remove ourselves from experiencing the benefits of this gift. When we place our will above his, we end up worshipping ourselves instead of the one true God. Second, intimacy with God flows from and is sustained by obeying his commands. In John 15, Jesus describes himself as the vine and us as the branches; we can only bear fruit by staying connected to him as the source of life. Jesus invites us to abide in his love just as he abides with the Father, offering us a profound connection that mirrors his intimacy with God the Father. Obedience, then, is the love language of heaven.

Men have a particular calling to lead, and obedience is the solid foundation of a life that fulfills this purpose. As a father of two boys, I want Donovan and Zeke to learn how to lead themselves, then lead others, and they can never do this without first learning how to submit to authority. My wife and I are teaching our sons how to be led so that, as they mature into men, they will understand that all good leadership is rooted in love.

Many young men chafe under the authority of someone else, whether that be their father, mother, coach, or teacher. We should not be surprised or scandalized when a boy asserts his own will, for this rebellious instinct was forged in mankind's original sinful disobedience. While expected, these expressions of immature independence should neither be celebrated nor ignored. Boys need their impulses evaluated, corrected, encouraged, and purified. Loving and intentional discipline helps young men thrive as they are given guardrails to help them stay on the path of virtue and greater holiness. Hebrews 12 affirms this: "For the Lord disciplines him whom he loves. . . . But he disciplines us for our good, that we may share his holiness. For the moment all discipline seems painful rather than pleasant; later it yields the peaceful fruit of righteousness to those who have been trained by it" (Hebrews 12:6, 10–11).

Allowing a boy to continue immoral behavior is not loving; neither is failing to set expectations and standards for him to meet. All discipline should originate from love, which is willing the good of the other. If love doesn't permeate the disciplinary moment, it can lead to shame and wounding. However, there's a big difference between unhealthy wounding that stems from an abusive relationship and the awkwardness and discomfort that accompany genuine disciplinary action. It's not fun for a father to hold his sons accountable, and very often they don't like it. However, their long-term growth requires us to rise above our own discomfort and choose to do what's right, even if we might prefer to look the other way.

My dad has always been my best friend. Very often, when given the option of having a friend from school or athletics join us for a family adventure, I'd decline because I simply preferred my dad. We laughed a lot, played constantly, and genuinely enjoyed each other. I would occasionally push his buttons or test the limits of his patience, but I generally wanted things to be good between us. This deep and beautiful friendship never superseded his responsibility to father me. I can think of plenty of times when I was disobedient, disrespectful, dishonest, or otherwise not living up to the standards my parents set for me. In those moments, Dad didn't pretend not to notice, minimize the seriousness of my mistake, or laugh it off. He would deal with me directly, firmly, and lovingly, but without undue consideration of my feelings. The threat of what my emotions might mean for our relationship moving forward was outweighed by his trust in the strength of our bond, which could withstand those times of disagreement or discord. As I became a father myself, I asked him about this dynamic, and he said, “Pete, I absolutely love being your friend, but I’m your father first.”

I learned to obey God because I had a father who showed me how. A man of God routinely turns to the Lord for guidance, perspective, and clarity. He does not fear what might be asked of him, because intimate and loving trust has been established between him and Jesus. He longs to please the Lord and trusts that whatever God wants is for his ultimate benefit. Even if that means moving to Ohio.

8

CULTIVATE VIRTUE

Be a good man, not a nice guy!

"Wake up, buddy!" My dad had the annoying superpower of being able to wake me up about three minutes before my alarm went off. No matter what time I set it, most mornings throughout high school began with his gentle but insistent encouragement to get out of bed. Often grumpily and begrudgingly, I would obey and wander into the den to pray with him. Over time, I learned to pray the Canticle of Zechariah with my eyes closed as I battled the urge to snooze a bit more.

One morning, instead of the usual psalms and prayers, Dad introduced a book he'd recently discovered and wanted to read together. Within a few chapters, both of us were captivated. Written by John Eldredge, *Wild at Heart* played a significant role in our understanding of what it means to be a godly Christian man. Over the subsequent years, we referred to it often, but the most profound lesson was the concept of being a good man instead of a nice guy. Eldredge supports the old adage that "nice guys finish last," and he offers a morally sound defense of why we're called not simply to be nice but to be good. Dad and I started playfully but seriously reminding each other, "Hey, you're not a nice guy . . . you're a good man." Both of us sincerely, although never perfectly, embraced this high call to goodness. Being "good" has many dimensions to explore, but one way to approach becoming a man of God is to strive to become a man of virtue.

There are two types of virtues in the Catholic faith: theological (faith, hope, and love) and cardinal (prudence, justice, fortitude, and temperance). All other virtues flow from these seven. While all are important and worth cultivating, I've noticed that two virtues in particular are often lacking in men today but were exemplified by my father. They are fortitude and meekness.

Fortitude, or courage, empowers a man to do what's right even in the face of hardship, danger, confusion, and weakness. It's an act of selflessness, whereby we willingly sacrifice our own concerns and needs for something greater. One of my favorite examples of this type of manly Christian courage is portrayed in Acts 7. Stephen has been brought before the Sanhedrin, and they give him the chance to defend himself. He bravely proclaims the truth about Jesus and culminates his speech with a very direct declaration: "You stiff-necked people, uncircumcised in heart and ears, you always resist the Holy Spirit" (Acts 7:51). Circumcision represented a covenant between God and the descendants of Abraham. It was a physical sign indicating a change of heart, the removal of sin, and commitment to God's laws. So, Stephen is making a bold accusation with these words, telling the Sanhedrin they have committed the grave error of turning their back on God. The scripture continues, "When they heard these things they were enraged, and they ground their teeth against him" (Acts 7:54). In other words, the Sanhedrin's response to Stephen's accusation was volcanic.

When our son, Zeke, was about three years old, he learned that he could express the emotion of anger. He would scrunch his face and grind his little teeth and say, "Grrrrr, I'm mad at you, Dad." In those moments, I was dying laughing on the inside, but as a good father, I had to stay in "dad mode." When a three-year-old boy grinds his teeth, it's generally pretty cute, but when a grown man grinds his teeth at another grown man, it's not cute—it's terrifying.

In the scripture, these men of the Sanhedrin have lost their minds with anger at Stephen. He is encountering a very real threat of danger because of his willingness to stand for the Gospel. This is what Christian manly courage looks like. Acts 7 recounts, "[Stephen], full of the Holy Spirit, gazed into heaven and saw the glory of God, and Jesus standing at the right hand of God;

and he said, 'Behold, I see the heavens opened, and the Son of man standing at the right hand of God'" (Acts 7:55–56). When fortitude is required, men of God are called to submit to the power of the Holy Spirit within them. The Spirit elevates our gaze to look beyond the worldly threat and recall God's heavenly promises. We can endure momentary discomfort—whether a splinter's pinprick or a dagger's agony—when our spirits are strengthened and emboldened to battle for eternal good. Like Stephen, our courage must be tied to a compelling *why*. In order to endure when things become difficult, we must be driven with clarity of purpose. Courage is not just something we feel or something we generate for ourselves; it is a supernatural strengthening in moments of trial—inspired by divine vision and noble cause—to equip us to do what's right, no matter the cost.

Often, the circumstances that demand courage from the modern man do not involve the battlefield or the public arena. Our families, communities, churches, schools, businesses, and marriages need men who have a clear moral vision of what is right and noble, and who possess the strength of character to pursue it, even when it proves difficult. A few years ago, I was helping my mom clean out some files and bins in her basement. While wading through boxes of old business articles, inspirational quotes, and chicken-scratch notes my dad had compiled over the years, I came across a file labeled "Family." In addition to some photos and keepsakes, it held a few letters my parents had written to my dad's mother, my grandmother. They were difficult yet inspiring to read. She had serious issues with alcohol that needed to be addressed, and my parents had the courage to lovingly acknowledge the problems and invite her to change. My mom proceeded to tell me the full story of those letters and the healing and restoration that eventually followed. Saying hard truths was the right thing to do.

If you come from a loving place, directly calling out the flaws you observe in another often results in that person immediately thanking you and choosing a new path. Just kidding. This rarely happens right away. People usually resist, fight back, take offense, hurl insults, or even make threats. Courageous men of God cannot take a definitive stand and then back down when they meet resistance. They must persevere and refuse to stop even when it gets hard. Initially, my grandma refused to quit drinking, which strained family relationships, but my dad remained patient and firm, because the noble cause of his mother's eventual health was worth the pain of confrontation.

Courageous men of God want to do what's right, persevere in the pursuit of it, and don't stop when it gets hard. This includes humbly accepting criticism or constructive feedback. To be courageous is not to ignore the possibility of making a mistake or the need to maintain virtuous flexibility when challenged. While the knee-jerk reaction might be to argue or to fight back, fortitude allows us to peacefully navigate those moments in the pursuit of a just and good outcome.

The second virtue I saw exemplified by my father is meekness. His meekness was not passivity, as a modern misunderstanding of this virtue might surmise. Rather, his meekness showed in his ability to temper and restrain his emotions such as the rare bouts of anger that inevitably erupt in the chests of all men at some point or another. Being meek meant his strength was under control.

As much as I respect, love, and genuinely like my mom, we've had arguments and battles for as long as I can remember. Whether about cleaning my room or agreeing on what movies I could watch, we would sometimes find ourselves arguing like a brother and sister more than a mother and son. I attribute this to our having so many of the same interests and personality quirks. However, after a particular episode when I was thirteen, I've never again taken for granted her God-given authority over me. We were bickering about something insignificant, and I started to get a little extra mouthy. Eventually, emotions got the better of me, and I decided to illustrate my point with a particularly ugly four-letter word. My dad, having seen this kind of disagreement before, had been a mostly disinterested bystander up to this point. As soon as he heard that word escape my mouth, he suddenly teleported across the room and grabbed the front of my shirt. I'll never forget the look on his face and the intensity in his voice as he stared directly into my eyes and said, “Son, don’t you *ever* speak to your mother like that again.”

He could have screamed. He could have even hit me. Instead, he controlled his power and let the seriousness of his words and tone express the depth of his righteous anger. Dad didn’t hesitate for fear that I wouldn’t like him or that he would hurt my feelings. He utilized his strength while maintaining complete control. The way he handled this episode taught me never to talk to my mom like that again, and I also learned how to be meek in my role as a man and, one day, as a husband and father.

A modern misunderstanding of this virtue might associate it with dullness or a lack of motivation. But meekness is neither weak nor insecure. Rather, the man who embodies meekness understands his strength and how to wield it. To be meek is to be humbly aware of your strength but have dominion over your power. Meekness flows from the cardinal virtue of temperance and, as such, is the antidote to unrighteous emotions.

Our current culture has little appreciation or understanding of kindness in its truest form. It’s not simply about being nice; it’s about cultivating genuine empathy and compassion for others. Instead, aggression, manipulation, and a selfishly competitive mode of interacting with others often receives recognition and celebration today. From social media to news media, a kind, self-controlled, and meek approach to conflict is usually overshadowed by bids to score rhetorical points and own the opponent. Even in tense disagreements that require a more aggressive approach to defending the good, the default disposition of a man of God should be oriented toward peace, humility, and the pursuit of outcomes that are best for everyone without descending into belittling, dismissiveness, and cruel attacks.

The second person of the Blessed Trinity has no shortage of power, yet Jesus describes himself in Matthew 11:29 as "meek and humble of heart" (NABRE). In doing so, he invites his followers to imitate his ability to wisely, peacefully, and gently control the strength that comes from faith. Even as he drove money changers from the temple, Jesus never lost control, keeping his incomparable strength directed toward the most loving outcome for all. Scripture tells us zeal for his Father's house consumed him, but this righteous anger was tempered with meekness.

The core of the virtuous life is the pursuit of holiness, becoming a man after God's own heart. With that in mind, don't forget that all of the actions attached to the virtuous disposition of our hearts must be grounded in, supported by, and directed toward love. The virtuous man loves as God loves, because God is love. None of the virtues achieve their full potential in our lives if we don't begin and end there.

A man of God embraces the daily call to live well, grow in virtue, and intentionally focus on areas of his life that need to improve and develop. He isn't preoccupied with being liked or unduly swayed by the affirmation and attention of others but instead derives purpose, meaning, and fulfillment from repeated good actions, words, and decisions. My dad loved people freely and without fear. His desire to bless others with his words and deeds did not stem from a superficial desire to be liked. Instead, he chose to love people—whether that meant supporting them or challenging them—to help them be better people and therefore closer to God. Our culture invites us to follow the wide and common road of being a nice guy. The Lord challenges us to the far more noble and narrow path of being a good and godly man whose face is set toward eternity.

9

PUT OTHERS FIRST

Welcome to the Dead Man's Club.

The two little vertical red lines appeared, and suddenly our tiny rental house was bursting with joy. We'd only been married for three months when we discovered Cait was pregnant with our first child. I was pumped. The desire to be a father like my dad had significantly influenced my vocational discernment toward marriage, and now the time had come.

Like many men, I just assumed we were having a boy. I'm a boy. I'm from a family of two boys. I had done ministry with boys. I figured God would want me to start with a son so he could be the leader of his siblings. Nine months later, the fateful day arrived, and we (actually, let's be honest, the effort was entirely my wife's) began the long journey of bringing our first child into the world. After more than thirty hours of heroic struggle, the baby emerged, and the doctor laid our child on my wife's stomach and said, "Okay, Dad, what do we have?" I looked down with great expectation and exclaimed, "Is that a girl?"

Not my finest moment, but the doctor patiently and somewhat condescendingly replied, "Umm, yes." Instantly, my desire for a boy evaporated as I was overcome with love for my daughter. My heart has never been the same. We didn't even have a girl's name picked out, but that didn't stop me from announcing the great news to my parents, who were holding vigil in the waiting room of the hospital. I burst through the double doors with my arms held high. "We have a beautiful, healthy baby . . . ," I paused for dramatic effect, " . . . girl!" Squeals of excitement erupted from my mom, while my dad smiled, grabbed me by the shoulders, and said, "Congratulations, son. Welcome to the Dead Man's Club."

Over the years, I came to appreciate my dad's unusual response as I changed blowout diapers at three in the morning, cleaned up incredible amounts of vomit, drove countless miles for sporting events, and saw our bank account ebb and flow with our children's needs.

You may have heard the slightly trite but apt saying "I am third," which represents the mindset that God is first, others are second, and I am third. As we mature, our instincts should evolve not only to recognize and serve the needs of those around us, but also to anticipate those needs. Observe nearly any high school boy when he returns home from a long day at school or practice, and you'll see evidence of the fact that boys tend to only notice and care about their immediate personal needs. If there's a bag of chips or a pint of ice cream within his sightline, it will be instantly consumed without a thought as to who else might want it, who bought it, or what other purpose it was supposed to serve.

With their hormones surging and brains still developing, young men are in a process of transformation, and a whole bunch of conflicting desires are vying for their attention. They want to be seen, known, valued, and chosen. They are also physically, emotionally, and sexually ravenous. They often want to both build and break things. The internet is full of videos of young men pulling pranks, pushing their limits, creating, experimenting, and pursuing epic physical endeavors. Boys love testing their strength and skill in a thrilling competition where victory and defeat hang in the balance. They are constantly measuring themselves against others they want to emulate, as an ever-present question lingers beneath the surface of their actions: *Am I enough?* Though this question focuses on the self, its answer can only be found through consistent self-gift. For it is only in giving that we can truly receive what God has to offer.

This question of worth is tied to our identity. If we believe that we're made for this world alone, we'll always be in want of the next material thing or earthly accolade to answer that nagging question. If we identify ourselves as anything but sons of God, we will always be searching for another balm to heal the ache of emptiness. Additionally, if our sense of worth is tied to what we do to prove ourselves versus what we sacrificially give, it's easy to let our egos and selfish desires become louder than God's call to be of service.

Growing up, I knew my dad worked hard and his jobs often required him to travel, but I never doubted his willingness and ability to provide for us. We lived a simple and comfortable life; nothing of necessity (aside from the occasional overpriced Nike basketball shoe) was out of reach. As I got older, I learned Dad had turned down several promotions and higher-paying new jobs because they would have required us to leave the Ann Arbor area. Mom and Dad had discerned early in their marriage that they wanted to raise their children near their families and root their lives in the remarkable Catholic community of Southeast Michigan. They prioritized family, community, and God's will over a bigger house, fancy cars, or even the ability to eat out regularly. Dad wasn't defined by his salary or job title, and as a result, he was able to make decisions that aligned with the flourishing of his marriage and family.

My dad's sacrifices came at the cost of material excess, but they created an environment for spiritual thriving for our family. As an adult, I look back in awe of the great lengths he went to in order to provide exactly what our family needed, but as a kid, I certainly don't recall thinking that I was observing anything extraordinary. He never complained about work or acted as though we were his financial burden to carry. Nor did he seek approval or celebration for the sacrifices he made for our family.

Boys have a natural desire for power and are fascinated with greatness. That's why the internet is bursting with debates about who's the GOAT and who's got the upper hand in every arena of life. It's not necessarily problematic for boys to look to admirable public figures in sports, business, or other secular areas for examples of how to reach certain steps on the way to their ultimate aspiration of holiness. It's important to be clear, though, about which traits are worthy of emulation and which do not honor God. For instance, some young men admire athletes who have achieved incredible physical feats, and they may therefore gravitate toward weight lifting as a means of fulfilling their desire to be capable and strong. This can be a good thing as long as it doesn't become the ultimate thing. Any personal effort, however noble, must always be rooted in the goal of self-sacrifice as a means of honoring God's will. If selfishness doesn't mature into selflessness, the pursuit of fulfilling any need or desire remains a self-determined effort.

Boys have to learn this truth through trial and error and the passing of years. When they're young, boys believe their lives are their own; they're the hero of their story and destined for worldly glory. They live for satisfaction, no matter how fleeting and without regard for reason or consequence. Tragically, many modern influencers validate this way of living. Flaunting wealth, physical fitness, and sexual conquest as evidence of their so-called worth, they acknowledge the base male desires for power and gluttonous fulfillment but fail to challenge men to sacrifice these selfish instincts and fulfill their true purpose by providing for others instead. Rather, they encourage their followers to pursue these immature feelings and disregard the inevitable destruction they'll leave in their wake.

In contrast, the most powerful example of masculine strength I've observed was also the most self-sacrificial. In my entire life, I only saw my dad drink one sip of alcohol; it was at my wedding because he lost a bet with my brother. He had long ago decided to fast from alcohol for his marriage. He loved chocolate, but I rarely saw him eat it. He decided to offer chocolate treats for his sons' purity. I was a virgin on my wedding night, and I believe the grace of his sacrifice aided my chastity and therefore strengthened the bond I still share with my wife today. Influencers flaunting ridiculous indulgences and adolescent attitudes online peddle the benefits of their selfish lifestyles, but I'd take the nearly forty years of faithful and joyful Catholic marriage that my dad shared with my mom over their money, cars, and clothes any day of the week.

The young men in our lives don't need more examples of selfish and self-indulgent behavior. They want to witness the heroism of the self-actualized man who, through the grace of God, has conquered his emotions and channeled his desires toward the flourishing of those around him. Jesus revealed that it is in giving that we receive and our Father will provide for our needs, so don't hold back. Radically pour out your life for the people Jesus has placed in front of you. You won't regret serving others, especially when you offer all of it to the Lord and ask him to bless your efforts with his love, joy, and peace.

The disordered subversion of masculinity that's all too often promoted today denies God's truth, which is that his gifts permeate all aspects of our lives when we do as Jesus instructed: "Seek first his kingdom and his righteousness, and all these things shall be yours as well" (Matthew 6:33). Men of God know this is true and strive to live in accord with this reality. They make decisions with their feelings and desires in mind but are not governed by them. I've heard it said that feelings are important companions on the journey of life, but horrible leaders.

My dad regularly lived in this rhythm. My brother and I knew that every day after dinner was playtime with Dad. It didn't matter if he was tired, frustrated by work, behind in his physical-fitness goals, or simply desiring to do something else; he always prioritized us after the meal. This meant creative basement games, evening golf matches, basketball in the driveway, or wrestling on the floor, but he always chose to provide what we needed, which was quality and quantity of time with him.

He also let our interests guide how we spent this recreational time with him. Both Brian and I were strong athletes. My dad, a former MVP of the University of Michigan baseball team, had high hopes that Brian would pursue a similar sports journey. But when Brian decided that he wanted to try his hand at other sports for a while, our dad didn't blink an eye. My brother eventually returned to baseball, and when we asked our dad about his willingness to let Brian explore other areas of interest, he replied, "If you had been really into butterfly catching, I would have found a way to join you in it!" Dad didn't believe that a father's personal wishes should unduly influence his child's spirit of curiosity or adventure. His role was to expose his son to a variety of opportunities, appreciate the passions his son discovered, and guide him toward success.

Our dad's willingness to put aside his personal passions and make himself a conduit for his sons' pursuit of theirs was one of the many ways he exemplified self-sacrifice. From his time to his treasure, our dad set aside his own desires and human instinct for self-preservation to better provide for our family, just as Jesus instructed in John 15:12–13: "This is my commandment, that you love one another as I have loved you. Greater love has no man than this, that a man lay down his life for his friends." Whether we find ourselves in the backyard or the basement or the boardroom, this is where we are being trained for heaven. We're learning how to sacrifice today so we can aim ever toward the eternity ahead.

10

EMBRACE SUFFERING

Go be with Jesus.

The doctor's apologetic, yet devastatingly clear prognosis hung in the air: "I'm sorry, but there's nothing more we can do." My dad, mom, and I were sitting in a hospital room on the seventh floor of the James Cancer Center in Columbus, Ohio. (Of all places for lifelong Michigan fans.) Here we grappled with the anticipated but now confirmed reality that Dad's cancer had progressed beyond treatment. The clinical study would be discontinued, and it was time to go home and make the final preparations for heaven. His doctor quietly left the room, and we sat there silently for several minutes. My eyes were trained on the carpet because I knew if I looked up at my hero, my strength would fail, and raw emotion would come pouring out. The silence was broken when he said quietly, "Pete, look at me." I immediately looked up, and tears filled both our eyes. He continued, "It's okay, son. I'm tired of fighting, and I'm ready to be with Jesus."

About a year earlier, I had gotten a call from my dad, which was not unusual since we talked on the phone nearly every day, but this one was different. He and my mom were in Washington, DC, at my cousin's college graduation, and he had just received the results from some tests ordered by his dermatologist. "Pete, I'm really sorry to tell you this, but I just got diagnosed with cancer." It wasn't just any cancer, but a particularly deadly and rare form called blastic plasmacytoid dendritic cell neoplasm, which we found annoying to remember, so we started calling it WAC, or Weird-Ass Cancer. Over the next several months, we went on the cancer journey too many others have traveled: intense chemotherapy, tracking blood counts, countless prayers, fear, hope, temporary remission, intentional family experiences, devastating cancer re-emergence, a new clinical trial, and ultimately the painful acceptance of hospice care.

As we drove home from Columbus on that fateful day, I remember marveling at my parents' strength, both in the Lord and in each other. Their beautiful marriage of thirty-nine years was coming to an end, and while they both felt deep sadness over the circumstances, neither despaired and neither's faith was shaken. The grace of the Sacrament of Marriage could be tangibly witnessed in their unwavering devotion to each other and their hope in Christ's gift of salvation.

A few weeks earlier, we had gone to Easter Sunday Mass together. We knew then that the clinical trial didn't seem to be working, and we were all struck by the harmony of celebrating Jesus's Resurrection and Dad's impending experience of that gift. When we got home from Mass, Dad settled into his favorite chair. A few minutes later, I noticed that he had become very still and basically zoned out. We attempted to get his attention, but he remained catatonic. Something was going on inside of him, and it looked serious. Eventually, through the loving presence of my mom and a gentle conversation with my aunt Martha, Dad came back and shared what had happened. He said he felt like the devil had made one last effort to pry him away from Jesus. Dad, facing his own mortality, was tempted to despair, to grasp at his earthly life and curse God for his deteriorating condition. He went into the valley of the shadow of death. The battle for his soul raged, but ultimately the Holy Spirit provided him the grace and power to cling to Jesus. We saw a shift in my dad that blessed Easter Sunday. He had spent his life preparing for heaven, and now he wanted to go.

A few days after our return from Columbus, we gathered around Dad's hospice bed. Earlier that day, our pastor had heard his final confession, anointed him, and prayed the Church's consoling and powerful end-of-life prayers. Now, my mom, brother, our wives, and a few family friends and relatives watched as Dad entered into his eternal reward. We sang songs, prayed the Rosary, told stories, quietly waited, and ultimately began to cheer Dad into heaven. I had the great privilege of holding his hand as he died. I looked at my lifelong hero, best friend, and father whose body had withered and suffered and remembered 2 Corinthians 4:16–17: "So we do not lose heart. Though our outer man is wasting away, our inner man is being renewed every day. For this slight momentary affliction is preparing us an eternal weight of glory beyond all comparison." My heart was broken, tears streamed down my face, but in my father's final earthly moments, I experienced an intense eruption of joy because I was so happy for him. Dad was with the One he loved the most. He had fought the good fight, finished the race, and received the prize of everlasting glory.

In the days after we lost my dad, I recalled how he had reacted in the aftermath of his own father's death. My grandfather and my dad loved each other deeply, and we all had a special relationship with Grandpa. I was eight years old and we were vacationing in Arizona when we got the call that Grandpa had died. My parents immediately brought us together to pray for his soul, for the comfort of my grandmother, and for God to be with us. Despite his emotional devastation, my dad's first instinct was to turn to the Lord for guidance. This was an identity-crisis moment. He had lost his dad and dear friend, and thus assumed the mantle of responsibility for the whole family. Despite how deeply unsettling it was to lose a parent, he turned to the Lord and asked him to lead the way.

And, now, it was time for me to do the same.

During my dad's illness, the following passage brought me great consolation:

> My son, if you come forward to serve the Lord,
> prepare yourself for temptation.
> Set your heart right and be steadfast,
> and do not be hasty in times of calamity.
> Cleave to him and do not depart,
> that you may be honored at the end of your life.
> Accept whatever is brought upon you,
> and in changes that humble you be patient.
> For gold is tested in the fire,
> and acceptable men in the furnace of humiliation.
> Trust in him, and he will help you;
> make your ways straight, and hope in him.
> (Sirach 2:1–6, RSV)

The pathway of following Jesus isn't guaranteed to be simple or smooth. We know Jesus helps us carry our crosses, but a cross remains an instrument of pain. It kills our earthly flesh so that our souls may be strengthened and ultimately renewed for heaven. Jesus never promised that following him would be painless, but he assures us that we will have intimacy with him in the struggle and spiritual fruit from persevering in trust. Each line of the Sirach passage speaks to how we are called to respond to this pain. Hold fast to the Lord, trust in his providence, focus on his will, and allow the fire of suffering to produce a positive outcome. No one reads "furnace of humiliation" and thinks, "That sounds awesome—sign me up!" Yet we know those moments are inevitable. We men need to ask ourselves: When I find myself in the fire, will I cry out to God, or will I run from him?

God has an opinion about every suffering. In some cases he may choose to heal and resolve things immediately and supernaturally. Other times he may utilize the passage of time, modern medicine, or the wisdom of others to bring relief. Some suffering will not be resolved until the joy and freedom of heaven. It's not our job to guess what he wants to do, but only to ask him for help, embrace his answer, and persevere in faith.

Jesus taught us how to suffer well. Very often, it's in times of trial that our growth in maturity and holiness is most evident. The true measure of a man is revealed through difficulties, disappointments, and challenges, because in those moments, there are fewer things to hide behind or be distracted by. Many of us lead very comfortable lives. We're blessed with easy access to food, central air conditioning, convenient transportation, and plenty of entertainment options. We can be lulled into a warped sense of comfort, where we become easily alarmed or unsettled when things aren't clean, quick, easy, or fun. However, we weren't made for this world that has shaped itself to our immediate desires. We are merely travelers here on the journey to heaven. This doesn't mean we can't enjoy the world we live in, but we should always live with a sense of healthy detachment, keeping all things in moderation. As James 4:14 reminds us, "You do not know about tomorrow. What is your life? For you are a mist that appears for a little time and then vanishes."

My dad embraced the wisdom of Sirach 2: "Accept whatever is brought upon you, and in changes that humble you be patient." If you've ever had the privilege of walking with someone as they die, you'll see many humbling changes. It can be awkward, uncomfortable, and frustrating, but my dad remained patient. Equipped with the supernatural grace Jesus offered him, he stayed steady on the path the Lord asked him to walk, rooted firmly in hope of heaven.

"Cleave to him and do not depart, that you may be honored at the end of your life." I wish you could have experienced my dad's funeral. Hundreds of people gathered to worship God and thank him for the gift of Chris Burak. The witness of Dad's life and his faithful death inspired several people to reconsider their perspectives on faith, and we know of at least one person who decided to come back to church after the funeral Mass. Each chapter of this book details a lesson I learned from my dad, but his last lesson might be the most important one. Dad showed us how to suffer with joy, trust the Lord no matter what, and persevere to the end.

CONCLUSION

In so many ways, my dad was extraordinary. And, in so many ways, he was very normal. Dad was a man of God. He pursued the Lord's will, surrendered to the Holy Spirit, and radically loved Jesus. Dad was completely and utterly devoted to my mom; they were best friends all the way to the end. He would have been uncomfortable that so much of this book is about him, since he considered his fatherhood to be completely united to my mom's motherhood. They were a team, through and through. Intentional, communicative, loving, joyful, and always in each other's corner. He worked hard every day to provide for his family. He loved golf, Michigan football, Motown music, and anything to do with his kids or grandkids.

I miss my dad every day. He's been gone for more than ten years, and there are still times when I reflexively think of things I can't wait to tell him (usually some silly thing the kids did or one of my harebrained business ideas). I recognize the painful irony that my own sons will never experience one of my dad's adventures, hear his infectious laugh, sing "The Victors" with him, or worship together at Christmas Eve Mass. At the time he died, Cait and I had two beautiful daughters, and one of the last things I said to Dad before he passed was "Dad, no rush, but when you get to heaven, we'd also really love a son." Just about nine months later, we welcomed Chris Donovan Burak to our family. Several other families have told us stories of asking his intercession for new babies. Many couples who struggled with infertility or miscarriages (as my parents did before conceiving my brother and me) are now joyfully adding healthy babies to their families. Each year, on May 28, we celebrate Papa Day (the grandkids called him Papa) with my mom and my brother's family. We tell stories about him often, ask for his heavenly help regularly, and strive to keep his legacy alive. Dad wasn't perfect, but you already knew that because nobody is, so don't be intimidated by the example he set. As I mentioned in the introduction, this book is designed to inspire, not to shame. My friends, whether you are a father yourself, a young man growing in maturity, a mom trying to understand her sons, or just someone who cares about young men, my dad and I want you to know, in no uncertain terms, that you are loved. It was his prayer and gift to me, and now it's my prayer for you.

ACKNOWLEDGMENTS

Just like forming boys into men, this book was a communal effort. Everyone on Team Burak came together to provide stories, commentary, affirmation, feedback, and motivation to share our family's stories and do it excellently. None of this would have been possible if my mom hadn't said yes to my dad all those years ago. Mom, you're a warrior, and I'm so grateful for your love, leadership, and walking with Dad through each of these rules.

Being a father myself has clarified these rules from my dad and been the most rewarding and challenging thing I've ever done. Cait, I love you and thank you for your unwavering devotion, support, joy, and deep faith. I *love* our life together, and it's only getting better. Gracie, Erin, Donovan, Zeke, and Regina, being your dad is an immense gift and privilege. Kids, who loves you?

My parents fostered a wonderful home life, and it worked because my older brother bought in first. Brian, thank you for your consistent affirmation, generous friendship, and wise perspective. Love you, man.

There are too many men who've invested in me over the years to adequately thank here. But the team at Renewal Ministries, and Peter Herbeck and Ralph Martin in particular, deserve a huge shoutout. Thank you for believing in me and giving me a place to radically respond to the Lord's call in my life.

Finally, a special thank you to the team at Ave Maria Press, especially Josh and Katie, for believing in this book and working incredibly hard and fast to make it happen.

Pete Burak is vice president of Renewal Ministries—an organization dedicated to renewal and evangelization in the Catholic Church—and codirector of Pine Hills Boys Camp. He also served as an EWTN host for coverage of the National Eucharistic Congress.

Burak earned a master's degree in theology from Sacred Heart Major Seminary in Detroit, Michigan. He writes a monthly syndicated column for the Diocese of Lansing's *Faith* magazine and has spoken at conferences throughout the United States and abroad on discipleship and evangelization, including SEEK, the Steubenville Power and Purpose Conference, the Legatus National Summit, and numerous men's and youth conferences.

Burak lives in Michigan with his wife and children.

renewalministries.net
Facebook: @pete.burak
Instagram: @peteburak
YouTube: @RenewalMinistries

Jake Khym is cofounder of Life Restoration Ministries, an apostolate dedicated to renewing the Church through healing, evangelization, and human formation, with a special focus on high-impact leaders. He also cohosts *Restore the Glory Podcast* with Bob Schuchts.

AVE

AVE MARIA PRESS

Founded in 1865, Ave Maria Press, a ministry of the Congregation of Holy Cross, is a Catholic publishing company that serves the spiritual and formative needs of the Church and its schools, institutions, and ministers; Christian individuals and families; and others seeking spiritual nourishment.

AVE | AVE MARIA PRESS
Notre Dame, IN
A Ministry of the United States Province of Holy Cross